## Guidelines for Photocopying Reproducible Pages

### Editorial Staff
**Senior Managing Editor,** Sheryl Haystead • **Senior Editor,** Debbie Barber • **Writer,** Joan Lansing-Eigenhuis • **Contributing Editors,** Allison Jolley, Lisa Key, Danette Starksen, Tracy Trexler • **Art Director,** Lenndy Pollard • **Designer,** Annette M. Chavez

**Founder,** Dr. Henrietta Mears • **Publisher,** William T. Greig • **Senior Consulting Publisher,** Dr. Elmer L. Towns • **Senior Consulting Editor,** Wesley Haystead, M.S.Ed.

Gospel Light's

# baby beginnings

## teacher's guide

### 18 to 36 months

Gospel Light

# CONTENTS

## CD-ROM Parent's Home Pages

**Parent's Home Pages—18 to 36 Months**
Introductory Parent's Home Page

| Year 1 | Year 2 |
| --- | --- |
| September | September |
| October | October |
| November | November |
| December | December |
| January | January |
| February | February |
| March | March |
| April | April |
| May | May |
| June | June |
| July | July |
| August | August |

# How to Use the Baby Beginnings Curriculum

## If You Are the Children's Pastor or Nursery Coordinator

• Prior to the start of each month, send home the appropriate month's overview (first two pages of each month's section) to each caregiver in the nursery.

• If you have a regular, consistent staff for the month, include the activity pages for the month as well and encourage your staff to plan together which activities they will prepare and provide each week of the month. (For example, one person would be prepared to lead a God's Wonders activity each week while another person would be prepared to lead an Active Play activity each week.)

• If you have a rotating staff, select several of the activities yourself. Collect any needed supplies and place them in the appropriate rooms along with the page of instructions (highlight or mark the activity). Alert the staff to look for these items when they arrive to serve.

## If You Are the Toddler/2s Classroom Coordinator or Teacher

• Each teacher in the classroom needs a copy of the monthly overview and activities. (Print out copies from the CD-ROM that comes with the *Baby Beginnings Teacher's Guide—18 to 36 Months*.)

• Teachers plan together which activities they will prepare and provide each week of the month. (For example, one person would be prepared to lead a God's Wonders activity each week while another person would be prepared to lead an Active Play activity each week.)

Note: Consider creating for each room a box for each month that contains the supplies for the month's learning activities as described in the *Baby Beginnings Teacher's Guides*. At the beginning of the month, the box is placed in the appropriate rooms for use by teachers.

**For Parents**
• Distribute a copy of the reproducible *I Love to Sing!* CD to each family.

• At the beginning of each month, send home (or ask your children's pastor to send home) both the appropriate month's *I Love to Look!* Bible Story Picture Card and *Parent's Home Page*. *Parent's Home Pages* are available on the CD-ROM that comes with this book, as well as in *Nursery Smart Pages*. Purchase one set of *I Love to Look!* Bible Story Pictures for each family.

# Teaching Toddlers

Somewhere between infancy and the preschool years, is the wonderful world of the toddler. God has made each child unique, and it is important to get to know each one, and their families, personally. Teachers should develop good communication with each family and learn about each child's strengths, challenges and needs. However, there are some characteristics that describe most typically developing toddlers. Taking these characteristics into account will make your teaching much more effective.

- Toddlers are active. They love to move and explore. They learn about the world by using all of their senses, by manipulating objects and by imitating the actions of others. Learning activities should involve things to look at, listen to, touch, smell and do.

- Toddlers live in the here and now. Make the most of "teachable moments" by connecting the curriculum learning aims to what a child is doing at the moment. Such guided conversations can help toddlers begin to understand spiritual concepts. For example, when a child offers a toy or comfort to another child, a teacher can say, "That was a very loving thing to do. Jesus wants us to love each other."

- Toddlers need close supervision. Their drive to explore may lead them to wander, climb, or do things they are not ready for. Some may still be putting fingers and objects in their mouths. It is important that everything in the toddler's environment is safe, too large to choke on and non-toxic.

- Toddlers want autonomy! They often use the word "no," even when they mean "yes." They may cry when their will is thwarted. Good teachers understand these feelings, while still setting and enforcing limits.

- Toddlers have difficulty waiting. It is important to have things ready for snack or other activities in order to minimize waiting. It is helpful to have more than one of a favored toy available.

- Toddlers' vocabularies are limited, but expanding rapidly. They understand more than they can articulate. A rich language environment is important, including adults who speak often and respectfully with them, and who listen and respond to what they say. Reading short, illustrated stories to toddlers will help expand their vocabularies.

- Toddlers have a short attention span. They will stay with an activity as long as they are interested. It is best to let them move to another activity when they are ready. When doing a group activity such as singing or moving to music, it is important to let toddlers join and leave the group as they choose. Stories work best when read to one or two toddlers at a time.

- Toddlers' concepts of God, Jesus, church, the Bible and prayer are very formative. They need adults who will demonstrate God's love and then connect that love to the name of Jesus. The concepts and stories in this curriculum have been chosen because they can be tied to children's own experiences. For example, when they see things that God has made and are told that God made them, toddlers' concepts of God begin to take shape.

- Toddlers have a short memory. Just because you said something once, do not expect toddlers to remember it later. Repetition of learning concepts, and classroom rules, is important.

Let the example of Jesus be your guide in relating to toddlers. The Bible tells us that He welcomed them even though He was very busy. He took them in His arms and blessed them. You can demonstrate the love of Jesus for His precious children with your loving words, your smile, and your touch.

# Loving and Guiding Toddlers

The heart of good teaching is relationships. It is important for teachers to form a relationship with each child in their class as well as with the child's family. Children respond more readily to guidance from those they love, and families are more open to input about their children if they know the teacher knows, understands and loves their children.

To build strong relationships with children and families, you can:

- **Pray** regularly for each child and family.
- **Give** parents a form to fill out requesting information about the child and family (see registration forms in *Nursery Smart Pages*).
- **Greet** each child and parent by name when they enter the classroom.
- **Express** your joy that they have come.
- **Ask** how their weekend is going to get an idea of how the child might be feeling.
- **Remember** the names of siblings and others important to the child and make reference to them.
- **Join** a child in a favorite activity.
- **Notice** and comment on pro-social behaviors. ("Thank you for sharing the play dough. That was kind.")
- **Assist** children when you sense they need help.
- **Comfort** children who are distressed.
- **Give** appropriate physical affection as you sense a child wants or needs it.
- **Follow** the child's lead in warming up to the classroom environment.
- **Tell** parents how the child's time in the classroom was spent, giving details that show you know their child. Be sure to tell parents about any event that might be upsetting to a child (getting hurt or frightened).

- **Call** or send notes to families when their children are absent.

Creating an age-appropriate environment will prevent many behavior problems from happening. To do this, you can:

- Make sure all toys, furniture and equipment are safe and child-sized.
- Store things that children should not touch out of their reach.
- Provide duplicates of popular toys.
- Carefully supervise all children at all times.
- Have enough adults available to respond quickly to children's needs.
- Avoid making children wait longer than necessary.
- Keep a consistent routine (the same activities in the same order), but be flexible with the time taken for each.
- Help children with transitions from one activity to another by giving them some warning and helping them do what you are asking (clean up toys, throw away trash, etc.).

To guide children's behavior in a way that is helpful, teachers must have realistic expectations of toddler behavior. These include:

- High levels of activity. Toddlers need space to move both indoors and out.
- Short attention spans. Toddlers need the freedom to change activities frequently on their own schedule.

- Short memory. Toddlers need frequent reminders of what is expected of them.
- Low tolerance for frustration. Toddlers may cry or lash out when they cannot have what they want.
- Self-centeredness. Toddlers have difficulty understanding the feelings and needs of others.
- Resistance to limits. Toddlers resist, but need, limits on their behavior.
- Limited ability to express themselves through language. Vocabulary is developing rapidly, but many children express themselves physically, especially when they are upset.
- Accidents and mistakes. Toddlers may spill their juice, wet themselves or break things.

Appropriate guidelines for toddlers include:

- Children should use gentle touches and kind words. They should not be allowed to hurt others with their bodies or their words. ("We say kind words." "I can't let you hurt our friends at church.")
- Children should use toys and materials appropriately. ("We need to roll the ball.")
- Children should be seated while eating and drinking. ("Here is the place for you to sit while you eat.")
- Children should walk when running might be dangerous. ("We need to walk when we're inside.")
- Children should obey their teachers' instructions. ("I need you to listen and do what I say. Thank you.")

Helpful teacher interventions when toddlers exceed limits include:

- Staying close enough to intervene when a child uses aggressive behaviors.
- Frequent reminders of what is expected. ("Touch your friend gently.")

- Expression of empathy. ("I know you want the toy, but Maria is having a turn.")
- Demonstration of appropriate behavior. ("We don't throw sand. Put it in the bucket like this.")
- Redirection to another activity. ("Jason is using the red truck. Let's see if we can find one for you.")
- Removal from a situation when inappropriate behavior persists. (A child who persists in throwing sand after reminding and demonstration should be removed from the sand area and encouraged to find another activity.)

If there is a child whose behavior consistently exceeds limits or harms others, ask teachers to observe the child and be ready to prevent or stop inappropriate behavior and to demonstrate appropriate behavior.

If the interventions above are not sufficient, the child's parents should be consulted.

Teachers should never:

- Use any type of physical punishment, including a slap on the hand.
- Shake a child.
- Raise their voices in anger.
- Deny food or beverage as a punishment.
- Deny physical activity as a punishment.
- Restrain a child, except for safety reasons.
- Use "time out" as a punishment. Children may need to be removed from an area until they calm down. The purpose should be to help the child.

- Use God as a way to control children's behavior (by saying things such as, "God doesn't like it when you do that").

Speaking with parents about their child's behavior will be easier if you have already built a good relationship with the family. However, you should not be surprised if parents respond defensively. Parents believe that their child's behavior reflects on their parenting abilities. The following ideas can make talking to parents go more smoothly:

- Pray for guidance before speaking to the parents.
- Consult a more experienced teacher or children's ministry staff person.
- Talk to parents in private, not when others are around to hear.
- Tell parents positive things about their child.
- Tell parents you have observed some behaviors that concern you.
- State the nature and frequency of the behaviors.
- Avoid using any labels ("hyper"), suggesting a diagnosis (ADHD), or making a value judgment ("aggressive").
- Ask parents if they have noticed the same behaviors at home. If they have, ask them how they handle it.

- Incorporate parents' suggestions, if appropriate.
- Invite the parents to observe in the classroom.
- Provide parenting classes for all families.

Special circumstances: Toddler behavior may be outside the norm in circumstances of family stress, such as divorce, moving, the birth of a new sibling or any other significant change in the family's life. Behavior should improve with time and loving support. Toddlers with identified developmental delays, allergies or other special needs may require extra support or alternate strategies to be successful in your classroom. This should be discussed with the parents, and teachers may need specialized training.

Remember that God made each child unique, with a unique temperament, personality and timetable of development. We have only a few glimpses in the Bible of Jesus' interactions with children. It is clear that children were important to Him. He made time for them while adults waited, He rebuked those who tried to keep them away, He took them in His arms and blessed them. The most important thing we can do for the toddlers in our care is bless them with our words and actions as Jesus would. They can begin to know the love of Jesus through our love. Love must be at the heart of our relationships with toddlers.

# Why Use Curriculum?

"These kids simply need to be fed, changed and played with . . . what can they possibly learn about God? Why would we need curriculum for them?"

First of all, our goal in using curriculum is not to get a child to spout theological concepts! Instead, our goal is to individually (one-on-one) teach each child through natural learning processes what he or she can begin to learn about God. Curriculum is designed to help you, the teacher, use the time you spend at church with little ones to build spiritual foundations.

Secondly, using curriculum also benefits you, the teacher, as much as the child. Singing and talking about Jesus is a powerful reminder that what you are doing is not just custodial care, but ministry in its truest sense. The same is true for parents. Just as young children need to hear about Jesus, their parents need to begin talking comfortably about Him with their child. The model the church provides of how we care for and "teach" children is intended to help parents catch on to the fact that they can and should do the same things at home.

Curriculum provides you with ideas and words that help make your natural teaching effective. Since the best kind of teaching for toddlers is primarily one-on-one, don't expect that these young children will sit in a circle or have a group time, or even remain interested in what you are doing for very long. But as you sit on the floor talking and playing with two or three children, make frequent use of the conversation ideas and songs suggested in your curriculum. Look for teachable moments—times when you can talk about the child's actions and connect them to the monthly theme. "Jocelyn, you used your hands to roll the red ball. God made your hands."

In every session, plan to provide several of the learning activities. Play portions of the CD, repeating the same songs frequently. The sounds, words, actions and most of all, the feelings that are created in this casual setting will flow into a natural pattern of teaching and learning that will eventually build a young child's understanding of God, Jesus and the loving comfort found in the people around him or her at church. And using a curriculum with monthly themes helps provide continuity to the activities in the nursery, especially when teachers change frequently.

In a large classroom where there are many children and adults in the same room, designate certain learning activities for each adult to provide for children throughout the session. For example, one teacher may position him- or herself on the floor with large cardboard blocks, building and talking about them with interested children. Another adult may sit near an open area of the room with a container of rhythm instruments, playing them and singing songs with children in that area of the room. However, as the session progresses, adults need to be ready to move to "where the action is." Flexibility is key.

A child's learning takes place all the time, as a natural part of living. So the teaching in your classroom is accomplished by your every look, word and act while you are in the presence of children. Your teaching is ministry just as surely as teaching a theology class for adults would be. This curriculum helps you to focus your playing, talking, caregiving, singing and finger plays in ways that familiarize a child with God's name and His love. Awareness of God's love for each child takes your time in the nursery far beyond the level of just singing "Itsy-Bitsy Spider" again!

# September

## I See God's Love at Church

### Jesus Came to Church
(See Luke 2:22-38.)

### "I like to come to church."
(See Psalm 122:1.)

**This month you will help each child:**

• hear songs and words about God's love;

• feel glad to be at church with people who demonstrate God's love to him or her;

• participate in enjoyable activities at church.

## Devotional

As you watch and learn from the children you teach, notice how anxious each one is for food to satisfy the pangs of hunger. No substitute will do! You may try distraction and play with toys, but a little one's requests for food will not stop until physical hunger is satisfied. This is one time when the child knows exactly what he or she needs.

Read 1 Peter 2:1-3. The apostle Peter urges us to have the same single-minded drive in satisfying our spiritual needs. Unfortunately, we often allow ourselves to be sidetracked. We try a wide variety of ways to find fulfillment or to eliminate problems. But our spiritual hunger continues, often making us as cranky as a hungry child! Peter tells us that only the pure milk of the word (see verse 2) can nourish the deepest needs of the human soul. Take time to be fed. Recognize the symptoms of your need and satisfy that hunger!

As a teacher, the gentle care you provide introduces young children to the nurture and love of the people who love God and His Son, the Lord Jesus. Your tasks may seem to involve only the physical care of changing, feeding, playing, cuddling and singing. However, those actions must be bathed in the warmth of Jesus' love. Such love will radiate from you as you take time each day to "taste" the goodness of the Lord (see Psalm 34:8). Just as children single-mindedly demand to be fed, demand "time out" from your busy schedule to feed your soul from God's abundant resources.

During the month of September, display this poster at child's eye level. Talk about the way in which the children in the poster are experiencing God's love at church by playing with toys and friends.

## I See God's Love at Church

### Do It!

#### I Come In

I come in,
there's a smile on my face.
I come in,
my friends are in this place.
I come in,
my friends say "hi" to me.
I'm in church,
what a happy place to be!

### Sing It!

#### It's Fun to Go to Church

(Tune: "Farmer in the Dell")

It's fun to go to church!
It's fun to go to church!
With all the other boys and girls
It's fun to go to church!

### Tell It!

#### Jesus Came to Church

When Jesus was a baby,
His parents brought Him to church.
People at church were
glad to see baby Jesus.
They talked to Him.
They smiled at Him.
They held Him close.
Jesus was happy to be at church.
You can be happy at church
Because people show God's
love to you here.
(See Luke 2:22-38.)

Display this poster at teacher's eye level in your nursery. Tell the Bible story, sing the song, do the finger play and repeat the Bible verse to one or more interested children.

## Activities with Children

Choose one or more of the learning activities on pages 11-16 to provide for children during a session. Consider your facility, the number of children and teachers and the supplies you have available as you plan which activities you will use. The best kind of teaching for toddlers will happen as you take advantage of teachable moments as children play and experience the learning activities you have provided. Continue an activity as long as one or more children are interested. For more information on using this curriculum, see "Why Use Curriculum?" on page 8.

## Building a Church

**Collect**

Toy construction tools (hammer, saw, etc.)
Cardboard boxes

**Do**

Use boxes and tools to "build" a church. Interested children may imitate your actions.

**Say**

God loves you, Seth.
I'm glad you came to our church today.
What is this tool used for?
I'm glad people built our church so we can come here and learn about God's love.

## Climbing *Steps* to Church

**Collect**

September Bible Story Picture from *I Love to Look!* or *Nursery Posters*
Child's step stool, or a large wooden block

**Do**

Show and talk about the Bible Story Picture.
Encourage children to go up and down the step stool, or to step on and off the wooden block.

**Say**

Jesus came to church. Mary and Joseph brought Him to church. The people at church loved Jesus.
Let's pretend we're going up the steps to church. We can see our friends at church.
I'm happy to see you at church today. God loves you!
At church we can learn about God's love.

## Driving to Church

**Collect**

Several age-appropriate ride-on toys (optional—child-sized chairs)

**Do**

Children ride on the toys, moving around the room as desired. (Optional: If ride-on toys are not available, arrange chairs to make a car. Children sit on chairs and pretend to drive.)

**Say**

Let's drive to church. Which car do you want to drive?
I'm glad we can come to church!
God loves you! People at church love you, too. Thank You, God, for the people at our church.

## Walking to Church

**Collect**

Masking tape

**Do**

Create a "path to church" on the floor of your room using the tape. Remove tape at end of session.
Demonstrate staying on the path while walking on it. Invite children to walk with you.

**Say**

Let's walk to church. Let's stay on the path together.
At church, we learn about God's love.
God loves you, Chloe.
**Bonus Idea:** Walk in different ways on the path (jump, tiptoe, etc.).

## People at Church

**Collect**

Marker

Construction paper shape or drawing of your church building for each child

Glue sticks

Pictures of people cut from magazines or catalogs

**Do**

Print "I see God's love at church" on shapes or drawings of church.

Child glues pictures onto church.

**Say**

I'm so glad you came to church today. At church we learn that God loves us.

Calvin, I'm happy to see you. People at church care about you.

## What Did You Wear to Church?

**Collect**

September Bible Story Picture from *I Love to Look!* or *Nursery Posters*.

Pieces of fabric in solid colors approximately 8 inches (20.5 cm) square

**Do**

Show and talk about the Bible Story Picture.

Spread fabric pieces on table or floor for children to see and touch.

Choose a piece that matches a child's shirt, dress, etc. and hold it next to the article of clothing.

**Say**

When Jesus was a baby, He came to church. Mary and Joseph brought Him to church. You came to church, too!

Devin, this cloth is blue, just like your shirt. You wore a blue shirt to church today.

I'm glad you're here. God loves you!

## Tire Track Roads

**Collect**

Length of butcher paper

Tape

Crayons

Toy cars with no small parts

**Do**

Tape butcher paper to top of child-sized table.

Let children use crayons to draw "roads" on the paper. Draw several roads yourself.

Children "drive" cars on the roads.

**Say**

I'm glad you came to church today. Marcus, how did you get here?

Some people drive to church. Some people walk.

I like to come to church. At church, I learn that God loves me.

## Church Windows

**Collect**

Pieces of colored tissue paper approximately 4 inches (10 cm) square

Masking tape

**Do**

Let children watch you tape tissue-paper pieces to a window, at child's eye level if possible.

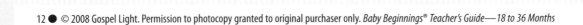

**Say**

Now our window has pretty colors. This paper is red.

Some churches have pretty colored windows.

We see God's love at church. Thank You, God, for our church.

## Nature Items

**Collect**

Variety of nature items (leaves, grass, shells, small branches)

**Do**

Set out nature items. Play a game like I Spy with children to help them identify and describe the items.

**Say**

I spy something green and skinny. Elton, what do you think it is? Yes, you pointed to the grass. God made grass. God loves us. At church we hear that God loves us.

I spy some seashells made by God. God loves us.

## I Am Loved at Church

**Collect**

Several pictures of babies and toddlers and several pictures of baby care items and toddler toys cut from magazines and laminated (or covered with clear Con-Tact paper)

**Do**

Invite children to help you match the pictures of the baby items to the pictures of babies and the toddler toys to pictures of toddlers.

**Say**

Where is the picture of the baby? Where is the picture of the rocking chair? We have rocking chairs at church for babies. People at church love babies.

Where is the picture of the little girl? Where is the picture of the blocks? We have blocks at church for you to play with. I love to play with you, too!

I'm glad we can come to church. We learn that God loves us.

## Who Came to Church Today?

**Collect**

September Bible Story Picture from *I Love to Look!* or *Nursery Posters*
Unbreakable mirror

**Do**

Show and talk about the Bible Story Picture.

Help one child at a time see his or her reflection in the mirror.

**Say**

Look at this picture of baby Jesus. He came to church. People at church loved baby Jesus.

Paloma, who is in the mirror? You came to church today. Mrs. Boyd came to church, too.

I'm glad you're here. God loves you!

## What Do You *See* at Church?

**Collect**

Toy binoculars, or make pretend ones out of two cardboard tubes

**Do**

Show a child how to look through the binoculars. As child looks around the room, describe what the child is seeing.

**Say**

I see my friend Kayley at church.

I see a picture of Jesus at church.

What do you see at church? We see our toys. We see people who love us. Thank You, God, for our church.

## God Loves Me

**Do**

Sing the following words to the tune of "Mary Had a Little Lamb":

God loves Nathan very much,
very much, very much.
God loves Nathan very much. I love Nathan, too.

**Say**

I know a song about how much God loves us. Let's sing it!

At church we learn about God's love. I'm glad we're at church together.

**Bonus Idea:** Play and sing along with "Together" from *I Love to Sing!* CD.

## Happy Band

**Collect**

September Bible Story Picture from *I Love to Look!* or *Nursery Posters*

*I Love to Sing!* CD and player

Variety of rhythm instruments

**Do**

Show and talk about the Bible Story Picture.

Give several children instruments. Hold one instrument yourself.

Play "A Happy Place." Children play instruments with the music.

**Say**

Do you see baby Jesus in this picture? He is at church. Mary and Joseph brought Jesus to church.

We're at church today. At church, we sing about God's love.

Alicia, I see that you are playing the bells. I'm glad you came to church to play the bells today.

Caleb, let's hear what the tambourine sounds like. God loves you!

## Walking to Church

**Collect**

*I Love to Sing!* CD and player

**Do**

Play "I See You!" and/or "Welcome." Encourage children to join you in walking around the room to the beat of the music.

Clap in time to the music as you walk.

**Say**

Let's pretend we are walking to church.

Marco, I'm glad you came to church today. God loves you.

## Making Music

**Collect**

Toy piano, toy keyboard or real electronic keyboard, or other musical toy

**Do**

Show one child at a time how to play the instrument.

Let child experiment with the instrument.

**Say**

We make music at church.

You can make music, too.

I'm glad you came to church. God loves you! Thank You, God, that Carl and Katie came to church today.

## Getting Ready for Church

**Collect**

Dolls

**Do**

Children pretend they are getting dolls ready for church.

Lead children to walk to another part of the room, pretending they are going to church.

**Say**

Let's get ready for church. We can bring our dolls to church today. Ready? Let's go!

I want to go to church to hear about God's love. People at church love you, Anna.

## Driving to Church

**Collect**

*I Love to Sing!* CD and player

Large cardboard blocks or boxes (optional—masking tape)

Small chairs

Plastic disc or sturdy paper plate for steering wheel

**Do**

Arrange blocks or boxes to be a vehicle. (Optional: Use masking tape to make a large rectangle on the floor representing a vehicle.) Place chairs inside vehicle.

Encourage children to get in the vehicle and sit on chairs. Let children take turns using the disc or plate to steer the vehicle.

As you "drive," play "A Happy Place" and sing along.

**Say**

Evan, how did you get to church today?

Let's build a car and drive to church. Who would like to be the driver?

I'm glad you came to church today. God loves you and so do I.

## My Bible

**Collect**

September Bible Story Picture from *I Love to Look!* or *Nursery Posters*

Several sturdy children's Bibles with pictures

**Do**

Set out Bibles for children to explore.

With an interested child, look at the Bible, talking about the pictures as you or child turns the pages. Show and talk about the Bible Story Picture.

**Say**

The Bible helps us learn about God's love. God loves everyone! God loves you, Brandy. Thank You, God, for loving us.

I see this picture of Jesus at church. Jesus went to church when He was a baby. People at church were glad to see Jesus. They loved Him.

## Block Play

**Collect**

Wooden or cardboard blocks (optional—jumbo interlocking blocks)

Toy cars and people (too large to swallow)

**Do**

Help children build a church and one or more houses with blocks.

Show children how to drive vehicles between church and home.

**Say**

Let's build a house. Who lives here?

Let's build a church. How can we get to our church from home?

I'm glad we can go to church to learn about God's love.

**Bonus Idea:** Make rectangular shapes on the floor with masking tape. Children stack blocks on tape to make houses.

## How Many Are Here?

**Collect**

September Bible Story Picture from *I Love to Look!* or *Nursery Posters*

**Do**

Show and talk about the Bible Story Picture.

Count aloud the number of children sitting or standing near each other.

**Say**

This picture shows baby Jesus at church. He is happy to be at church. Let's count how many people are in this picture. There are five!

I see three children who came to church today. Ella, Brendan and Evan came to church. I'm glad you are all here.

God loves all of you and so do I. Thank You, God, for Your love.

## God Loves Me

**Collect**

8½x11-inch (21.5x28-cm) sheet of paper for each child

Marker

Stickers

**Do**

Print the words "God loves (child's name)" on each paper.

Let children decorate their papers by placing stickers on the papers, any way they like.

**Say**

God loves you, Natalie.

At church, we learn about God's love.

I'm so glad that God loves Natalie. I'm so glad that God loves James.

**Bonus Idea:** Let children hold and look at a Bible. Say, "The Bible tells us that God loves us."

## Puzzles

**Collect**

Several toddler puzzles

**Do**

Let children play with puzzles. Talk with children about God's love.

**Say**

Carlos, can you find where the ball goes in this puzzle?

It's fun to play with you. People at church love you, Carlos.

I'm glad you're here today. I love you and God loves you, too.

## People Come to Church

**Collect**

Toy people

Shoe box with a flap cut on one side

**Do**

Show children how to "walk" people into the "church." Then set items on a child-sized table or the floor for children to play with.

**Say**

The boy is going to church. Now the girl is going to church.

You came to church today. I'm glad to see you! God loves you.

**Bonus Idea:** Use wooden or cardboard blocks to build a simple structure.

# October

## Jesus Loves Children

### Jesus Loved the Little Children
(See Mark 10:13-16.)

### "Jesus loves the children."
(See Mark 10:16.)

**This month you will help each child:**
- hear songs and words about Jesus' love for children;
- feel loved by caring teachers;
- participate in play activities that teach him or her about Jesus' love.

## Devotional

What does it mean to become like a child? How can an adult humble him- or herself to be childlike?

These questions must have gone through the minds of some of Jesus' disciples when He set a child in their midst in answer to their question about who is greatest. Read Matthew 18:1-4. This formula for greatness with the emphasis on little children sounded quite contrary to all the commonly accepted ideas about status. Perhaps as the disciples looked at the child Jesus had recruited for His object lesson, they began to see some of the qualities of the child that Jesus valued.

As you observe the young children in your church, one of the first characteristics you may notice is their total dependence on others. Surely Jesus was calling attention to our dependence on God. How often do we impair our effectiveness by thinking we can get by with just our own ability! What new horizons of growth might become visible to us if we could see beyond the limits of our own resources to what God has made available to us?

What other valuable childlike qualities can you nurture in your own life? Perhaps the openness of an infant should be cultivated? Might not the child's demonstrations of affection be good examples to imitate? What if adults showed a young child's desire to learn? Carefully watch a child during the next session. Look for attributes in that child for you to imitate spiritually. It's the path to greatness!

During the month of October, display this poster at child's eye level. Talk about the child in the poster and Jesus' love for all children.

## Jesus Loves Children

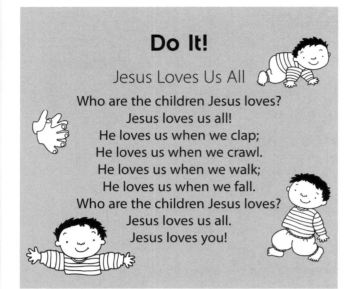

### Do It!

#### Jesus Loves Us All

Who are the children Jesus loves?
Jesus loves us all!
He loves us when we clap;
He loves us when we crawl.
He loves us when we walk;
He loves us when we fall.
Who are the children Jesus loves?
Jesus loves us all.
Jesus loves you!

### Tell It!

#### Jesus Loved the Little Children

Jesus loved the little children.
Mommies and Daddies
brought their children to Jesus.
Jesus held the little babies close.
Big boys and girls walked to
Him all by themselves!
Jesus smiled at all the children.
And the children smiled at Him.
Some children came and sat near Jesus.
Some children climbed
right up in His lap!
Jesus loved each one.
(See Mark 10:13-16.)

### Sing It!

#### Each Little Child

(Tune: "Mary Had a Little Lamb")

Jesus loves each little child,
Little child, little child.
Jesus loves each little child,
He loves you, yes, He does.

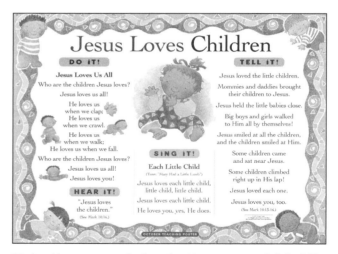

Display this poster at teacher's eye level in your nursery. Tell the Bible story, sing the song, do the finger play and repeat the Bible verse to one or more interested children.

## Jesus Loves Children

Choose one or more of the learning activities on pages 19-24 to provide for children during a session. Consider your facility, the number of children and teachers and the supplies you have available as you plan which activities you will use. The best kind of teaching for toddlers will happen as you take advantage of teachable moments as children play and experience the learning activities you have provided. Continue an activity as long as one or more children are interested. For more information on using this curriculum, see "Why Use Curriculum?" on page 8.

## Climb the Hill

**Collect**

October Bible Story Picture from *I Love to Look!* or *Nursery Posters*

Several large pillows

**Do**

Show and talk about the Bible Story Picture.

Arrange the pillows on the floor to make a "hill." Children crawl to "climb" over the "hill."

**Say**

Look at this picture. One day some children went to see Jesus. Maybe they had to walk up a hill.

Who would like to climb our pillow hill?

Jesus was happy to see the children. Jesus loves children.

## Roll the Ball

**Collect**

Medium-sized rubber or plastic ball

**Do**

Invite two or three interested children to sit on the floor with you.

Roll the ball to each child in turn, saying, "Jesus loves (child's name)."

**Say**

Jesus loves children. Jesus loves you, Annissa.

We're having fun playing together. I'm glad to know that Jesus loves us.

## Beanbag Toss

**Collect**

Laundry basket or other container

Several beanbags

**Do**

Show children how to toss beanbag into basket or other container.

Children take turns tossing beanbags.

**Say**

Penni, I see that you are tossing the beanbag. Jesus loves Penni.

Sophie can toss the beanbag, too. Jesus loves you.

Jesus loves children.

**Bonus Idea:** Using blocks and large sheet of cardboard, build a ramp. Children roll balls down ramp.

## Jump for Joy

**Collect**

Hula hoop

**Do**

Lay the hoop on the floor.

Demonstrate stepping into the hoop and jumping and invite children to follow your example. Some children may not be able to jump yet.

**Say**

Tiana is in the hoop. Jesus loves Tiana.

Will is learning to jump. He is having fun! Jesus loves Will.

Thank You, Jesus, for Your love.

## Jesus Loves Children Picture

**Collect**

Magazine pictures of children
Glue sticks
Construction or drawing paper with "Jesus Loves Children" printed at the top

**Do**

Children glue magazine pictures to paper. Show children how to put glue on back of pictures.

**Say**

Let's make pictures about Jesus' love. These words say "Jesus Loves Children." Jesus loves all children.

Jesus loves you, Liane. Which picture would you like to glue on this paper?

## Leaf Rubbings

**Collect**

Leaves with interesting shapes
Construction or drawing paper
Masking tape
Large crayons, with paper removed

**Do**

Help each child select a leaf and place it face-down under a sheet of paper.

Tape paper to table.

Child rubs side of crayon over paper to make leaf appear. Repeat process if child is interested. Use different leaves and crayon colors if desired.

**Say**

What color is your leaf, Alexandra? What color crayon will you use? You are making pretty leaf drawings. Jesus loves you.

I see one, two, three children making leaf drawings today. Jesus loves all the children. Jesus loves you!

**Bonus Idea:** Take a walk with the children to collect the leaves.

## Smiley Faces

**Collect**

October Bible Story Picture from *I Love to Look!* or *Nursery Posters*
9x12-inch (23x30.5-cm) sheet of construction paper for each child
Crayons

**Do**

Before class, draw a large smiley face on each sheet of paper.

In class, show and talk about the Bible Story Picture. Children color smiley faces.

**Say**

Here is a picture of Jesus and some children. One day some children came to see Jesus. Jesus was happy to see them. Jesus showed how much He loved them. Jesus loves you!

Casey, look at the smiley face! It makes us happy to know that Jesus loves us.

## People Play Dough

**Note:** This activity is best used with children over the age of two.

**Collect**

Commercial or homemade non-toxic play dough
Fabric sheet or tarp
Masking tape
People-shaped cookie cutters
Small rolling pins or 1-inch (2.5-cm) diameter dowel cut in 6-inch (15-cm) lengths

**Do**

Before class, tape sheet or tarp to floor under a child-sized table.

In class, children play with dough, and use cookie cutters if interested. Carefully watch to be sure that children do not eat dough.

**Say**

Who would like to make a person with their play dough? Abby, is your person a boy or girl?

Jesus loves boys. Jesus loves girls.

## Exploring Apples

**Note:** Post a note alerting parents to the use of food. Also, check children's registration forms for possible food allergies.

### Collect
Several washed apples of different varieties
Knife (keep out of reach of children)
Cutting surface
Optional—premoistened towelettes

### Do
Before class, peel and cut some of the apples into very small pieces.

In class, wash children's and your hands (optional—use towelettes). Talk about the color of the apples.

Cut an apple open and show children the seeds. Give children pieces to taste.

### Say
We're eating good apples together.

I'm glad we're together! Jesus loves us. Jesus loves children.

Jesus makes good food grow for us to eat.

## Comparing Leaves

### Collect
Variety of fall leaves
At least one magnifying glass

### Do
Display leaves where children can look at and touch them.

Let children use the magnifying glass to examine leaves.

### Say
Gerardo, you are looking at a big green leaf. Here is a leaf that is red.

Leaves come from trees Jesus made. Thank You, Jesus, for the leaves.

Jesus loves us. Jesus loves children.

**Bonus Idea:** Collect other child-safe nature items (small pumpkins, dried corn cobs, gourds, etc.) for children to see and touch.

## Jesus Loves You

### Collect
October Bible Story Picture from *I Love to Look!* or *Nursery Posters*
Unbreakable hand-held mirror

### Do
Show and talk about the Bible Story Picture.

Show a child his or her reflection in the mirror.

### Say
This picture shows Jesus and some children. One day some children came to see Jesus. Jesus loved them and was glad to see them.

Let's see who Jesus loves—it's Vanessa!

Jesus loves you.

## Pumpkin Muffins

**Note:** Post a note alerting parents to the use of food. Also, check children's registration forms for possible food allergies.

### Collect
Pumpkin (or other) muffins cut into bite-size pieces
Small paper plate or large napkin for each child
Optional—premoistened towelettes

### Do
Wash children's and your hands (optional—use towelettes).

Serve muffins to children.

### Say
Who would like to eat a special treat?

Olivia, I'm glad you are here today. Jesus loves you, Olivia. Jesus loves children.

Jesus helps us have good food to eat.

## Song: Jesus Loves Children

**Collect**

October Bible Story Picture from *I Love to Look!* or *Nursery Posters*

**Do**

Show and talk about the Bible Story Picture. Sing the following words to the tune of "Are You Sleeping?":

> Jesus loves children.
> Jesus loves children.
> He loves you. He loves me.
> Thank You, thank You, Jesus.
> Thank You, thank You, Jesus,
> For Your love, for Your love.

**Say**

Look at this picture of Jesus and the children. When some children came to see Jesus, He was glad to see them. Jesus showed the children how much He loved them.

I'm glad Jesus loves children. I love children, too!

We can thank Jesus for loving us. Thank You, Jesus, for Your love.

## Shake High, Shake Low

**Collect**

*I Love to Sing!* CD and player

Rhythm instruments such as shakers, tambourines or rattles made with gourds

**Do**

Give each interested child an instrument.

As you play "We're Special," lead children in shaking instruments high and low.

Say the rhyme below, standing still and moving as directed.

> Shake your rattle high
>   (*stand in place*).
> Shake your rattle low
>   (*stand in place*).
> Jesus loves you wherever
>   you go (*walk in place*).

**Say**

Kenna, which instrument do you want? It's fun to play these instruments.

Jesus loves you when you play. Jesus loves you when you make music.

Jesus loves all the children.

## Walking to See Jesus

**Collect**

*I Love to Sing!* CD (or other recorded music with a marching beat) and player

**Do**

Play "Watch Me!" or other music and lead children in stomping, waving, walking, running, crawling as desired.

**Say**

Some children went to see Jesus one day. Maybe they walked. Maybe they ran. Maybe they crawled.

Jesus was happy to see them. Jesus loves children.

Fernando, Jesus loves you.

## Dancing to Music

**Collect**

*I Love to Sing!* CD (or other recorded music with a lively beat) and player

Scarves in a variety of colors

**Do**

Give each child a scarf. Play "I Can Do!" or other music and invite children to dance or move around the room, waving their scarves.

**Say**

I'm happy because Jesus loves me. Jesus loves you, too.

When we're happy, we feel like dancing. Who would like to dance with me? Here's a scarf for you, Henry.

**Bonus Idea:** Provide other materials for children to wave: lengths of ribbons, crepe paper streamers, ribbon batons, etc.

## Jesus Loves Children of All Colors

**Collect**

Dolls of different ethnicities

Baby care items (doll bed, baby blankets, etc.)

**Do**

Children play with dolls and care for them.

**Say**

Some children have dark skin. Some children have light skin. Jesus loves all children. Jesus loves you. (Note: Children don't notice ethnic differences before age two.)

Leticia, how can you take care of and show love to this baby?

## Block Play

**Collect**

October Bible Story Picture from *I Love to Look!* or *Nursery Posters*

Large, soft blocks

Toy people (too large to choke on)

**Do**

Show and talk about the Bible Story Picture.

Let children play with blocks and people freely.

**Say**

Liam, can you point to Jesus in this picture? That's right! Jesus loves children. These children were glad to see Jesus. Jesus was glad to see them, too!

Mommies and daddies love their children, too. Jesus loves you. Thank You, Jesus, for Your love.

## How Do You Feel?

**Collect**

Paper plates

Large craft sticks

Duct tape

Markers

**Do**

Before class, make paper plate masks by cutting eye holes and attaching sticks to chin area. Draw a happy face, an angry face and a sad face on separate masks.

In class, show children the masks and hold one up to your face.

Allow children to play with the masks if they choose to.

**Say**

This child is sad. Carlos, Jesus loves you when you're sad. I love you, too.

Here is the mask with an angry face. Jesus loves you when you're angry.

Jesus loves us all the time.

## Packing Up

**Collect**

One or more small backpacks

Variety of toys

**Do**

Children pack and unpack toys in the backpacks. Talk about Jesus' love for us everywhere we go.

**Say**

Miles, I see that you are putting the toy people in your backpack. Where are you going to go? Jesus loves you at the park. Jesus loves you wherever you go.

Jesus loves all children. Jesus loves you.

## Jesus and the Children

**Collect**

October Bible Story Picture from *I Love to Look!* or *Nursery Posters*

A sturdy Bible storybook with pictures and simple text telling about Jesus, including if possible the story of Jesus and the children

**Do**

Invite one or two children to look at the book and Bible Story Picture with you.

Read the story and ask children to point to pictures of Jesus, children, etc.

**Say**

One day some children came to see Jesus. Jesus was happy to see the children. Jesus loves children.

Jesus loves you. Jesus loves all the children. Thank You, Jesus, for Your love.

## People Puppets

**Collect**

Children hand puppets

**Do**

Show children how to use the puppets.

Help children put puppets on their hands.

Use one puppet yourself to talk to child (see suggestions below).

**Say**

Hi, my name is Susan. Would you like to play?

Jesus loves us when we play. Jesus loves us when we are asleep.

Jesus loves you, Kyle.

## Matching Faces

**Collect**

Matching sets of children's faces (use duplicate sets of digital pictures of your children's faces or make duplicate photos from magazines)

Laminating equipment or clear Con-Tact paper

**Do**

Before class, laminate the pictures or cover them with clear Con-Tact paper.

In class, spread pictures out on table.

Invite interested children to find two identical pictures.

**Say**

Jesus loves children. Let's find some children Jesus loves.

Jesus loves Garrett. Jesus loves Maria.

**Bonus Idea:** Lead children to say names of children aloud with you.

## Puzzles

**Collect**

One or more toddler puzzles depicting children

**Do**

Show a child a puzzle and talk about the children in it.

Invite the child to take the puzzle apart and put it back together. Help child as needed.

**Say**

Adriana, look at this puzzle. These children are playing in the sand.

Jesus loves you when you are playing. Jesus loves you when you are riding in the car.

# November

## God Gives Me Food

**Jesus Gave Food to His Friends**
(See John 21:9-13.)

**"God gives us food."**
(See Genesis 1:29.)

• • • • • • • • • • • •

**This month you will help each child:**
• hear words and songs about God's gift of food;
• feel thankful for good food;
• taste and identify several foods.

## Devotional

After fishing all night, Jesus' disciples should have needed no coaxing to begin eating. Yet there they stood on the beach, dumbfounded that their Lord who had recently risen from the dead, made two miraculous appearances in locked rooms, and produced an abundant catch of fish from previously sterile water was now standing beside a fire, cooking their breakfast. Read John 21:9-13.

As the disciples stood there, Jesus served their food. He knew that His earthly ministry was quickly drawing to a close. He knew He must give great attention to preparing the disciples for their coming responsibility. Nevertheless, Jesus took time for a simple act of kindness to meet a basic physical need. When we meet the basic needs of young children, we are a reflection of Jesus' kindness.

Have you recently recounted the needs in your life that Jesus has helped you meet? What problems has He helped you cope with successfully? What challenge has He helped you to meet? What burdens has He helped make lighter? And then, have you thanked Him for the many ways in which He has helped you? Scripture reminds us, "Do not be anxious about anything, but in everything, by prayer and petition, with thanksgiving, present your requests to God. And the peace of God, which transcends all understanding, will guard your hearts and your minds in Christ Jesus" (Philippians 4:6-7).

During the month of November, display this poster at child's eye level. Talk about the child in the poster and express thankfulness for the good food God helps us have.

## Do It!

### My Food

This is my nose
To smell my cracker.
These are my eyes
To see my cracker.
These are my hands
To hold my cracker.
This is my tongue
To taste my cracker.
Thank You, God,
For my cracker.

## Tell It!

### Jesus Gave Food to His Friends

Jesus' friends were hungry.
So Jesus cooked some fish and bread.
"Come and eat!" Jesus said.
The fish and bread tasted good.
Jesus' friends were glad
He gave them food.
We are glad for our food, too.
(See John 21:9-13.)

## Sing It!

### I Thank God

(Tune: "Mulberry Bush")

Apples taste so good to me,
So good to me, so good to me.
Apples taste so good to me.
I thank God for my food.

Display this poster at teacher's eye level in your nursery. Tell the Bible story, sing the song, do the finger play and repeat the Bible verse to one or more interested children.

## Activities with Children

Choose one or more of the learning activities on pages 27-32 to provide for children during a session. Consider your facility, the number of children and teachers and the supplies you have available as you plan which activities you will use. The best kind of teaching for toddlers will happen as you take advantage of teachable moments as children play and experience the learning activities you have provided. Continue an activity as long as one or more children are interested. For more information on using this curriculum, see "Why Use Curriculum?" on page 8.

## Let's Be Farm Animals

**Collect**

Sturdy book with pictures of farm animals

**Do**

Look at books with children.

Show children how to move and sound like farm different animals. Encourage them to join you.

**Say**

God made cows. Cows give us milk.

God loves us. God helps us have good food to eat.

Xavier, which animal do you want to be?

## Gathering Eggs

**Collect**

Several baskets with handles

Several dozen plastic eggs

**Do**

Place the eggs around the room.

Children find eggs and place them in baskets.

**Say**

God made chickens. Chickens give us eggs. God gives us good food.

I like to eat scrambled eggs. I'm glad God gives us good food to eat.

Thank You, God, for giving us food.

**Bonus Idea:** (Post a note alerting parents to the use of food. Also, check children's registration forms for possible food allergies.) Prepare real, hard-cooked eggs. After they are collected, peel them for children to eat.

## Picking Fruit

**Collect**

November Bible Story Picture from *I Love to Look!* or *Nursery Posters*

Pictures of fruit (laminated or covered with clear Con-Tact paper) or toy fruit

Removable tape

Large basket

**Do**

Before class, tape fruit pictures at various levels around the room, or set toy fruit around the room.

In class, show and talk about the Bible story.

Encourage children to "pick" the fruit and put it in the basket.

**Say**

This picture shows Jesus and His friends. Jesus helped His friends have food to eat. They ate breakfast together.

Aiden, I see that you are picking an apple. You can put the apple in your basket. God made apples. God gives us good food to eat.

Is this an apple or a banana? This apple is red. Apples taste so good. I like to eat bananas, too. Bananas are yellow.

God gives us good food to eat. God loves us.

## Going to the Store

**Collect**

Paper or canvas grocery sacks

Variety of play grocery items, or real grocery items that have been discarded and cleaned

**Do**

Set the grocery items on a table or shelves.

Let children "buy" grocery items by placing them in sacks.

Children pretend to take groceries "home" and remove from sacks.

**Say**

God made such good food for us to eat.

Let's pretend we're going grocery shopping. Daniel, do you want to buy some cereal or some eggs?

I like to eat soup and sandwiches. Thank You, God, for giving us good food.

**Bonus Idea:** Provide a toy cash register for children to use.

## Placemat

### Collect
Pictures of food cut from magazines or grocery store ads, at least three or four for each child (Note: Pictures should be at least 2x3-inches (5x7.5-cm) in size.)

Glue sticks

12x18-inch (30.5x45.5-cm) sheet of construction paper for each child

Clear Con-Tact paper

Scissors

### Do
Print the words, "God gives (child's name) food" at the top of the paper.

Show children how to put glue on back of a picture and stick it to the placemat. Children choose several pictures and glue them onto placemats.

When child is finished with placemat, put clear Con-Tact paper over it to protect it from food spills. Child takes placemat home.

### Say
God gives us good food to eat because He loves us.

Jerome, what do you like to eat?

**Bonus Idea:** Give children food or seasonal stickers to add to their placemats.

## Spicy Smells

### Collect
November Bible Story Picture from *I Love to Look!* or *Nursery Posters*

Several spices (cinnamon, nutmeg, etc.)

Resealable plastic bags

### Do
Before class, put a small amount of each spice into a plastic bag.

Show and talk about the Bible Story Picture.

Open bags to let children smell spices as desired.

### Say
What are Jesus and His friends doing? They are eating breakfast. Jesus cooked some fish for them to eat. Jesus helped His friends have good food to eat. You're glad to have good food, too.

Logan, can you smell something good in this bag? This smell reminds us of good food God gives us to eat.

Emma, what food do you like to eat?

## Apple Prints

### Collect
White construction paper

Red, green and yellow crayons

### Do
Children color. Talk about how God made red, green and yellow apples.

### Say
Nicole, you are coloring with the red crayon. I like to eat red apples. God made apples.

God gives us good food to eat. Thank You, God, for apples.

## Tasting Cereal

**Note:** Post a note alerting parents to the use of food. Also, check children's registration forms for possible food allergies.

### Collect
Three or four healthy cereals made with different grains, such as O-shaped oat cereal, puffed rice, and corn flakes

Small plastic or paper serving bowls

Small bowl or paper napkin for each child

### Do
Place each type of cereal in a separate serving bowl.

Tell children the name of each cereal and give them a taste. Give them more cereal on request.

### Say
This cereal is made from corn. Bella, would you like to taste it?

God gives us good food to eat. God loves us!

We eat cereal for breakfast. What else do you like to eat for breakfast?

## Where Fruit Grows

### Collect

November Bible Story Picture from *I Love to Look!* or *Nursery Posters*

Several pieces of fruit (if possible, provide fruit attached to a branch)

### Do

Show and talk about the Bible Story Picture.

Display fruit on a child-sized table. Let children handle the fruit and talk about it.

### Say

This picture shows Jesus and His friends. They are eating some cooked fish. Jesus loved His friends. He helped them have good food to eat.

God made many kinds of food for us to eat.

Oranges grow on trees. God made fruit trees to give us food.

God gives us good food to eat.

## Pudding

**Note:** Post a note alerting parents to the use of food. Also, check children's registration forms for possible food allergies.

### Collect

Vanilla pudding (purchased or prepared before class)

Small paper cup and spoon for each child

Optional—premoistened towelettes

### Do

Wash your hands and the children's hands. (Optional: Use towelettes.)

Serve small amounts of pudding to children.

### Say

Milk comes from cows that God made.

God gives us good food to eat. God loves us. Thank You, God, for milk and pudding.

**Bonus Idea:** Add several banana slices to children's pudding.

## Tasting Fruit

**Note:** Post a note alerting parents to the use of food. Also, check children's registration forms for possible food allergies.

### Collect

Three or four different fruits (apples, bananas, oranges, grapes)

Knife (keep away from children) and cutting surface

Napkins

Optional—premoistened towelettes

### Do

Wash your hands and the children's hands. (Optional: Use towelettes.)

Show children the fruit and let them touch and smell the fruit. Tell children names of fruit and help them describe the fruit.

Cut fruit into very small pieces for children to taste.

### Say

God gives us food to eat because He loves us.

This red apple is crunchy. I'm glad God gives us good food to eat.

## Where Carrots Grow

**Note:** Post a note alerting parents to the use of food. Also, check children's registration forms for possible food allergies.

### Collect

Some whole carrots with tops still on

Grater

Bowl

Optional—premoistened towelettes

### Do

Wash your hands and the children's hands. (Optional: Use towelettes.)

Let children handle carrots and tops. Talk about where the carrot grew.

Help child safely grate a few carrot shavings to taste.

### Say

This carrot grew in the ground.

God gives us good food to eat.

Elton, God loves you.

## Food Container Drums

### Collect

*I Love to Sing!* CD and player

Empty food containers suitable for making drums

Light-colored construction paper cut to fit around drums

Tape

Stickers (depicting different foods if possible)

### Do

Ask child to select a container for his or her drum. Talk about the food that came in the container.

Help child cover the container using construction paper and tape. Encourage child to decorate drum with food stickers.

Children tap drums with hands while listening to "Thank You."

### Say

Jasmine, what kind of food came in this can? I like to eat beans.

God gives us good food to eat. God loves us.

## Rice Shakers

### Collect

November Bible Story Picture from *I Love to Look!* or *Nursery Posters*

*I Love to Sing!* CD (or other recorded music with a lively beat) and player

Several small, clean, empty water bottles

Uncooked rice

Duct tape

### Do

Before class, pour one tablespoon of rice into each water bottle. Screw cap on tightly. Secure with duct tape.

In class, show and talk about the Bible Story Picture.

Children use shakers while "Thank You" or other music plays.

### Say

Here is a picture of Jesus and His friends. One day Jesus helped His friends have good food to eat. They ate breakfast together.

Many people eat rice. Rice tastes good!

God gives us good food to eat. I'm glad we can eat good food every day.

**Bonus Idea:** Post a note alerting parents to the use of food. Also, check children's registration forms for possible food allergies. Serve children some cooked rice.

## God Gives Me Food

### Do

Ask children what kind of food they like.

Sing the following words to the tune of "God Is So Good," substituting foods children name for "food":

God gives me food.  God gives me food.
God gives me food.  He's so good to me.

### Say

God gives us good food. Let's sing about that.

Madeline, you said that you like to eat raisins and ice cream. God gives us food like raisins and ice cream. God loves you.

## Driving to the Store

### Collect

*I Love to Sing!* CD and player

### Do

Ask children what they like to buy at the grocery store.

Guide interested children to "drive" around the room while "Food for Me" is playing.

### Say

Let's pretend we are driving to the store to buy some milk. Here we go!

God gives us such good food to eat. Let's go to the store to buy some bread.

God gives us good food because He loves us. Thank You, God!

## Grocery Store

**Collect**

Empty food containers

Paper bags with handles (smaller than grocery store bags)

Cash register and toy grocery carts, if available

**Do**

Put food containers on child-sized tables or large boxes.

Give each child a bag. Let children "shop" for food.

**Say**

God loves you. He gives you good food to eat.

Juan, I see you are putting some cereal in your bag. I'm glad God gives us cereal to eat.

## Restaurant

**Collect**

Child-sized table and chairs

Centerpiece (flowers in plastic vase, candle, etc.)

Tablecloth

Play food and dishes

Optional—picture menus (glue several pictures of food on paper and laminate or cover with clear Con-Tact paper)

**Do**

Help children arrange restaurant items.

Children pretend to eat at restaurant. Model saying "please" and "thank you."

**Say**

It's fun to eat in a restaurant. At restaurants we can eat good food. God made good food for us to eat.

God gives us good food because He loves us. Thank You, God, for good food.

## Thanksgiving Dinner

**Note:** Post a note alerting parents to the use of food. Also, check children's registration forms for possible food allergies.

**Collect**

November Bible Story Picture from *I Love to Look!* or *Nursery Posters*

Tablecloth

Seasonal paper plates and napkins

Finger foods, cut small enough to avoid choking, such as apple slices, turkey slices, cheese cubes

**Do**

Show and talk about the Bible Story Picture.

Let children help set the table. Pray, thanking God for food.

Let children select foods to taste.

**Say**

Kayla, look at this picture. Jesus and His friends are eating at the beach. Jesus' friends were glad to eat good food. Jesus loved His friends.

God gives us good food to eat. I like to eat turkey for our Thanksgiving Dinner.

Anthony, you are eating good food. God loves you and gives you good food to eat.

## Going on a Picnic

**Note:** Post a note alerting parents to the use of food. Also, check children's registration forms for possible food allergies.

**Collect**

Large basket or paper bag

Real food and drink

Blanket

**Do**

Let interested children help put picnic items in basket or bag.

Go outdoors, if possible, or spread blanket on floor for picnic.

Pray, thanking God for food. Eat food together.

**Say**

Jesus ate food with His friends.

I'm glad God gave us food to eat today. Thank You, God, for good food.

**Bonus Idea:** Give each child a small paper sack. Each child puts one picnic item into his or her sack.

## Food Match

### Collect

Pictures (from magazines or Internet) of several foods and their sources, such as milk and cow, fruit and fruit tree, etc.

### Do

Before class, laminate pictures or cover with clear Con-Tact paper.

In class, help children match each food to its source.

### Say

Milk comes from cows. Calvin, can you find the picture of the cow?

God gives us good food to eat.

God loves you.

## Surprise Pictures

### Collect

Large manila envelope

9x12-inch (23x30.5-cm) sheets of construction paper

Magazine pictures of foods (as large as possible)

Glue

### Do

Before class, glue pictures of foods onto separate sheets of paper. Place papers into the envelope.

In class, hold up the envelope and slowly pull out one sheet of paper at a time.

Children identify foods pictured.

### Say

Mckenna, what food do you see in this picture? You're right! It's some strawberries.

God gives us good food. God loves us.

Thank You, God, for the food You made.

## Can You Find the Food?

### Collect

Large tray on which you have placed several toy foods that children will recognize (bread slice, tomato, apple, etc.)

### Do

Name a food and ask a child to point to it. Repeat with each food.

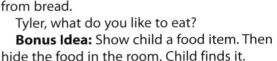

### Say

God loves you.

He gives you bread to eat. I like to eat sandwiches made from bread.

Tyler, what do you like to eat?

**Bonus Idea:** Show child a food item. Then hide the food in the room. Child finds it.

## Magnet Fishing

### Collect

November Bible Story Picture from *I Love to Look!* or *Nursery Posters*

Pictures (from magazines or Internet) of fish and shellfish used for food

Paper clips

12-inch (30.5-cm) dowel (or a ruler)

12-inch (30.5-cm) piece of string

Large magnet

Bucket or dishpan

### Do

Before class, laminate the pictures or cover them with clear Con-Tact paper. Attach a paper clip to each one at the mouth. Make a fishing pole by tying the string to the dowel and tying the magnet to the end of the string.

In class, show and talk about the Bible Story Picture. Place fish in bucket or pan.

Show child how to "catch" the fish with the pole. Name each fish that is caught.

### Say

Here is a picture of Jesus and His friends. One day Jesus cooked breakfast for His friends. Jesus gave them fish to eat. His friends were glad to eat good food.

I'm glad to eat good food, too.

God gives us good food to eat. God loves us.

# December

## Jesus Was a Baby

### Jesus Was Born
(See Luke 2:4-7.)

### "His name is Jesus."
(See Luke 1:31.)

• • • • • • • • • • • •

**This month you will help each child:**
• hear words and songs about the birth of Jesus;
• feel glad that Jesus was born;
• play with toys and materials to learn about the birth of Jesus.

## Devotional

There was never a birth announcement to equal it! On a nearby hillside angels were proclaiming joy, salvation and peace. In a faraway land, a group of wise men were stunned by the appearance of a star.

Immediately after hearing the news, the shepherds rushed into Bethlehem; the wise men began to plan for their trek westward. The accounts in Luke and Matthew reflect great excitement and joy. Read the accounts of their journeys in Matthew 2:1-12 and Luke 2:4-20. But what followed the first flush of emotion, the awe and wonder of the event?

The shepherds returned to their hillside, continuing their daily rounds of herding the flocks. The wise men faced an arduous journey through strange and possibly dangerous lands. And Mary and Joseph faced the daily routines of caring for an infant. The excitement lasted only a short time, then the familiar patterns of normal life were resumed. But even though the angel choir was gone, "Mary treasured . . . all these things . . . in her heart" (Luke 2:19).

December may be filled with much excitement for your family and church. However, in the midst of the celebrations, take time to treasure the presence of Christ in daily living. Set aside moments to ponder the ways He touches your life with joy, salvation and peace.

During the month of December, display this poster at child's eye level. Talk about the items in the poster which remind us of Jesus' birth.

## Do It!

### Look into the Stable

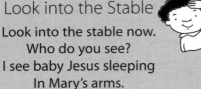

Look into the stable now.
Who do you see?
I see baby Jesus sleeping
In Mary's arms.

Look into the stable now.
What do you hear?
I hear baby Jesus laughing
In Joseph's arms.

## Sing It!

### Happy Birthday, Jesus!

(Tune: "Jesus Loves Me")

It's Jesus' birthday, time to sing!
Shake the bells and make them ring.
Let's all sing a happy song.
Bring your drums and march along.

Happy birthday, Jesus,
happy birthday, Jesus,
Happy birthday, Jesus.
We sing this happy song.

## Tell It!

### Jesus Was Born

Mary held her baby.
Her baby's name was Jesus.
She rocked Him gently in her arms
And sang a quiet song to Him.
Joseph held baby Jesus
And watched Him wiggle and laugh.
All through every day, and
all through every night,
Mary and Joseph loved and
cared for baby Jesus.
We are glad baby Jesus was born.
(See Luke 2:4-7.)

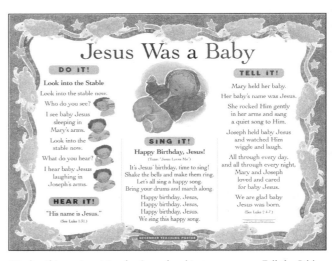

Display this poster at teacher's eye level in your nursery. Tell the Bible story, sing the song, do the finger play and repeat the Bible verse to one or more interested children.

## Activities with Children

Choose one or more of the learning activities on pages 35-40 to provide for children during a session. Consider your facility, the number of children and teachers and the supplies you have available as you plan which activities you will use. The best kind of teaching for toddlers will happen as you take advantage of teachable moments as children play and experience the learning activities you have provided. Continue an activity as long as one or more children are interested. For more information on using this curriculum, see "Why Use Curriculum?" on page 8.

## Walking to Bethlehem

**Collect**

December Bible Story Picture from *I Love to Look!* or *Nursery Posters*

**Do**

Show and talk about the Bible Story Picture. Take children for a walk around the room.

**Say**

This picture shows baby Jesus. Jesus was born in Bethlehem. Mary was Jesus' mother. Mary and Joseph loved and cared for baby Jesus.

Let's pretend we are walking to Bethlehem, like Mary and Joseph.

I'm glad Jesus was born. Thank You, God, for Jesus.

## Follow the Shepherd

**Collect**

Scarf
Stretchy headband or narrow length of fabric
Optional—walking stick

**Do**

Fasten scarf around your head with headband or fabric length to make a Bible times headpiece. (Optional: Carry the walking stick.)

Pretend to be a shepherd and lead interested children as sheep on a walk around the classroom.

**Say**

I'm dressed like a shepherd. A shepherd takes care of sheep. Who would like to be my sheep?

What sound does a sheep make? Natalie, can you follow me and make sheep sounds?

Some shepherds went to see baby Jesus when He was born.

## Find the Baby

**Collect**

Baby doll wrapped in a blanket

**Do**

Hide the baby in different places around the room, accessible to children.

**Say**

Can you find the baby doll in our room? The shepherds went to find baby Jesus. I'm glad Jesus was born!

## Follow the Star

**Collect**

Yellow or white construction paper
Scissors
Tape
One or two flashlights

**Do**

Before class, cut large star shapes out of the paper. Tape stars on walls or ceiling of your room.

Let children help you shine the flashlight on the stars.

**Say**

Can you see the star? Katie, God put a bright star in the sky when Jesus was born.

Some men followed the star to find Jesus. They were glad Jesus was born. I'm glad Jesus was born, too!

## Nativity Pictures

**Collect**

9x12-inch (23x30.5-cm) sheet of construction paper for each child

Set of nativity stickers for each child

**Do**

Help children put stickers on paper any way they choose.

Name the people and items as they are placed on the paper.

**Say**

This is baby Jesus. I'm glad Jesus was born. Madison, can you point to baby Jesus' mother?

Jesus was born in a stable. A stable is a barn where animals live.

Morgan, what animal is this?

**Bonus Idea:** Help children glue four craft sticks onto the paper in the shape of a stable.

## Play with Hay

**Note:** Post a note alerting parents to the use of hay. Also, check children's registration forms for possible allergies.

**Collect**

December Bible Story Picture from *I Love to Look!* or *Nursery Posters*

Container (dishpan size or larger)

Hay or straw (may be purchased at craft stores)

Toy farm animals (too large to choke on)

**Do**

Show and talk about the Bible Story Picture.

Cover bottom of container with a layer of straw. Place animals on top of straw.

Children play with animals.

**Say**

Look at this picture. Do you see the animals in the stable? A stable is like a barn where animals live. Jesus was born in a stable with animals. There is lots of straw in a stable.

How does this straw feel? Straw helps the animals stay warm and dry.

I'm glad Jesus was born. Thank You, God, for Jesus.

## Bathing Babies

**Collect**

Two dishpans with a small amount of slightly soapy water

Two or more washable plastic dolls

Towels

Two small washcloths

**Do**

Set each dishpan on a towel.

Show children how to wash dolls. Invite them to do it. (Optional: Instead of dishpans, have children pretend to wash dolls, or give them wet washcloths to use in their pretend play.)

Use additional towels to clean up spills.

**Say**

Ella, who gives you a bath? Your grandma takes good care of you.

Mary and Joseph took good care of baby Jesus.

Jesus was a baby.

## Star Scenes

**Collect**

9x12-inch (23x30.5-cm) dark blue construction paper sheet for each child

Star stickers

Yellow crayons and/or white and yellow jumbo chalk

**Do**

Children put star stickers and draw marks for "stars" on their papers.

**Say**

This is a star. God put a special star in the sky when Jesus was born.

This is a tree. Do you have a Christmas tree at your house? Jesus was born at Christmas.

We're glad that Jesus was born.

## Sheep Skin

### Collect

December Bible Story Picture from *I Love to Look!* or *Nursery Posters*

Sturdy book with pictures of sheep

One or more pieces of real or imitation sheep skin (fabric, car seat cover, etc.)

### Do

Place sheep skin(s), books and picture on a child-sized table. Show and talk about the pictures.

Invite a child to feel the sheep skin.

### Say

Lily, point to the sheep in this picture. Jesus was born in a stable. A stable is where animals like sheep live.

This wool came from a sheep. Sheep have wool to keep them warm.

I'm glad Jesus was born. Jesus was born at Christmas. Thank You, God, for Christmas.

## Star Gazing

### Collect

Ruler

Scissors

Four or more cardboard tubes

Dark blue or black construction paper

Masking tape

A push pin

### Do

Before class, cut a 3-inch (7.5-cm) circle from the construction paper for each tube. Cut 12½-inch (31.8-cm) slits around the edge of the circle (see sketch a). Cover the end of each tube with the circle and tape it in place. Poke six to eight holes in the paper (see sketch b). Tape two tubes together to make a viewer.

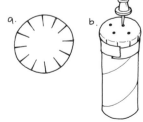

In class, show child how to hold viewer toward light and look to see "stars."

### Say

Can you see the lights? They look like stars.

God put a special star in the sky when Jesus was born.

Jesus was born at Christmas. We're glad Jesus was born!

## Christmas Touch 'N Feel

**Note:** Post a note alerting parents to the use of pine tree or branches. Also, check children's registration forms for possible allergies.

### Collect

Small pine tree or branch

### Do

Place tree or branch on a child-sized table.

### Say

This is a real pine tree. Can you feel it? Can you smell it?

These are called needles.

Do you have a Christmas tree at your house? At Christmas we remember that Jesus was born. I'm glad Jesus was born.

**Bonus Idea:** Provide pinecones for children to see and touch.

## Baby Visit

### Do

Before class, ask a mom or dad with a small baby to visit your class.

In class, let children look at the baby and gently pat him or her. Talk with children about the baby.

### Say

This is baby Anthony. Can he talk? Can he walk? What can baby Anthony do?

God gave him a mommy and daddy to take care of him.

Jesus was a baby. Mary and Joseph took good care of baby Jesus.

## Christmas Bells

**Collect**

*I Love to Sing!* CD and player

Jingle bell instrument for each child (optional—large bells strung on chenille wire circle)

**Do**

Play "Christmas Party."

Let each child choose an instrument. Children shake the bells with the music.

**Say**

Christmas is a happy time. Jesus was born at Christmas.

I see Cade shaking his bells. I see Alexandra shaking her bells. We're glad Jesus was born.

Thank You, God, for baby Jesus.

## Mary Rode to Bethlehem

**Collect**

Sturdy book with pictures of Mary and Joseph traveling to Bethlehem

**Do**

Show pictures to an interested child.

Sing the following song to the tune of "Mary Had a Little Lamb":

> Mary rode to Bethlehem,
> Bethlehem, Bethlehem.
> Mary rode to Bethlehem,
> on a little donkey.

> Joseph walked to Bethlehem,
> Bethlehem, Bethlehem.
> Joseph walked to Bethlehem,
> beside the little donkey.

> Jesus was born in Bethlehem,
> Bethlehem, Bethlehem.
> Jesus was born in Bethlehem,
> as a little baby.

**Say**

Can you point to the picture of Mary? Can you point to the picture of Joseph? They are riding a donkey and walking to Bethlehem.

Jesus was born in Bethlehem. I'm so glad!

**Bonus Idea:** Provide one or more toy rocking horses for children to ride on while you sing this song.

## Rock the Baby

**Collect**

*I Love to Sing!* CD (or other recorded lullaby) and player

Several baby dolls

**Do**

Play "Baby Jesus" or other lullaby.

Children rock baby dolls.

Sing along with the music.

**Say**

Babies like to be rocked. When Jesus was a baby, His mother rocked Him.

Jesus' mother was glad Jesus was born. We are glad that Jesus was born, too!

Jesus was born at Christmas.

## Christmas Music

**Collect**

December Bible Story Picture from *I Love to Look!* or *Nursery Posters*

*I Love to Sing!* CD (or other recorded children's Christmas music) and player

**Do**

Show and talk about the Bible Story Picture.

Play "Christmas Party" or other music while children play.

**Say**

This picture shows baby Jesus, Mary and Joseph. Mary and Joseph loved and cared for baby Jesus. I'm glad that Jesus was born.

Let's sing a Christmas song about baby Jesus. Jesus was born at Christmas.

Thank You, God, for Jesus.

**Bonus Idea:** Give children child-safe nativity figures to play with and arrange during this song.

## The Christmas Story

**Collect**

December Bible Story Picture from *I Love to Look!* or *Nursery Posters*

Toy or stuffed animals (sheep, cow, donkey)

**Do**

Show and talk about the Bible Story Picture. Children play with animals.

**Say**

Look at this picture to see Mary, Joseph and baby Jesus. Mary took good care of baby Jesus. When Jesus was born, some shepherds went to see Him.

A shepherd takes care of sheep. Who wants to take care of these sheep?

The shepherds were glad Jesus was born. I'm glad, too!

## Decorate the Tree

**Collect**

Unbreakable ornaments (stars, bells, nativity figures, etc.)

Optional—ornament hangers, artificial tree (about 3 feet [.9 m] tall)

**Do**

Children play with ornaments. (Optional: Children decorate tree.)

**Say**

Here is a star ornament. God put a star in the sky when Jesus was born. I'm glad Jesus was born.

Will, look at this bell ornament. We ring bells to show that we are happy Jesus was born.

## Caring for Babies

**Collect**

Several baby dolls and baby blankets

Baby care items such as doll bed, child-sized rocking chair, baby bottles and doll clothes

**Do**

Children take care of "babies," rocking them, feeding them and dressing them.

**Say**

Let's wrap the baby in a blanket to keep her warm.

Mary wrapped baby Jesus in warm clothes. Mary was glad Jesus was born. I'm glad, too.

This baby is hungry. Let's give him some milk.

## Wrapping Presents

**Collect**

Tissue paper

Tape

Stick-on bows

**Do**

Place items on a child-sized table.

Encourage children to find "presents" (toys) to wrap up. Be available to help as needed.

**Say**

Would you like to wrap a present? When Jesus was born, some men brought special presents to Jesus. The men were glad Jesus was born.

Giving and getting presents at Christmas makes us glad. Jesus was born at Christmas. Thank You, God, for Jesus.

**Bonus Idea:** Give each child a small gift such as a book or ornament related to Jesus' birth.

## Nativity Set

**Collect**

One or more child-safe nativity sets with pieces too large for choking

**Do**

Children arrange and play with nativity figures.

**Say**

Brandy, where is the baby? His name is Jesus. Kenna, where is the baby's mother? Her name is Mary.

I see a cow. Benjamin, what sound does a cow make? Jesus was born in a place where animals live.

## Christmas Box Match

**Collect**

Four shoeboxes (or other boxes) and lids, each box and lid wrapped in a different Christmas wrapping paper

**Do**

Set out boxes and lids. Show children how to remove and replace lids.

Let children match lids and boxes.

**Say**

At Christmas we give and get presents. Jesus was born at Christmas. Our presents show how glad we are that Jesus was born.

Bella, what toy do you want in your present?

I'm glad to give presents at Christmas. I'm glad Jesus was a baby.

**Bonus Idea:** Put toys inside boxes.

## Christmas Cups

**Collect**

Seasonal paper cups (two sets)
Toy people (too large for choking)

**Do**

Place cups on floor or child-sized table. Children match cups.

Turn cups upside down and put a toy person under each cup. Children turn over cups to find the people.

**Say**

Riley, you found the little boy in the red cup. What is under the Christmas tree cup?

These cups remind us of the time when Jesus was born. Jesus was born at Christmas. People were glad that Jesus was born. I'm glad, too!

## Christmas Story

**Collect**

December Bible Story Picture from *I Love to Look!* or *Nursery Posters*

One or more sturdy picture books telling the story of Jesus' birth

**Do**

Look at the pictures with children. If children are interested, read the story to one or two children at a time.

Talk about the pictures.

**Say**

I'm glad Jesus was born. Jordan, can you find the picture that shows baby Jesus? Who else is in the picture?

Jesus was born at Christmas. Thank You, God, for Jesus.

# January

## God Helps Me to Grow

**Jesus Grew**
(See Luke 2:52.)

**"God made us."**
(See Malachi 2:10.)

**This month you will help each child:**

• hear words and songs about the way in which Jesus grew;

• feel thankful that God is helping him or her to grow;

• experience opportunities to demonstrate new accomplishments.

## Devotional

Read Luke 2:21-40. Mary and Joseph must have closely observed their infant son in the days and weeks following their visit to the Temple. The prophecies of Anna and Simeon, added to the previous announcements by angels, undoubtedly stirred expectations of unusual qualities in their child. Would this child with such a special destiny show special abilities at an early age?

If Mary and Joseph had anticipated some dramatic evidence of Jesus' divine nature in the early years of His life, they must have been disappointed. After the excitement of the prophecies, life settled back into normal routines. Jesus gradually began to mature. The Gospels do not record any amazing intelligence, precocious abilities, or supernatural authority. Like all young children, He simply continued to grow. Gradually, daily, He kept increasing "in wisdom and stature, and in favor with God and men" (Luke 2:52).

When we discover significant insights or have dramatic spiritual experiences, we often expect that life will suddenly become different. We are frequently disappointed that the impact of Sunday seems so weak on Monday. We would like to reach maturity in large, bold moves. We become impatient with the slow, small steps that seem to make so little difference.

Yet as Jesus grew normally through all the stages of infancy, childhood and adolescence, Scripture assures us the grace of God was upon Him (see Luke 2:40). That same grace works today in each Christian's heart and mind, guiding the gradual but powerful process of growth, as we seek to become more like Jesus.

During the month of January, display this poster at child's eye level. Talk about the baby and the girl in the poster and how God helps children grow.

## Do It!

### I'm Growing

When I was a baby,
I was very, very small.
Now I'm growing older.
I'm growing big and tall.

When I was a baby,
I could only crawl.
Now I can walk, and I can jump.
But, sometimes, down I fall!

## Sing It!

### I Am Growing

(Tune: "Are You Sleeping?")

I am growing.
I am growing.
Yes, I am.
Yes, I am.
One time I was smaller.
Now I am much taller.
Watch me grow.
Watch me grow.

## Tell It!

### Jesus Grew

Once Jesus was a baby.
Jesus learned to crawl.
Then He learned to walk.
Jesus grew to be a bigger boy.
He learned to do many things.
You are growing, too.
You are learning to talk and sing and run
and climb.
God made you.
God will help you grow.
(See Luke 2:52.)

Display this poster at teacher's eye level in your nursery. Tell the Bible story, sing the song, do the finger play and repeat the Bible verse to one or more interested children.

## Activities with Children

Choose one or more of the learning activities on pages 43-48 to provide for children during a session. Consider your facility, the number of children and teachers and the supplies you have available as you plan which activities you will use. The best kind of teaching for toddlers will happen as you take advantage of teachable moments as children play and experience the learning activities you have provided. Continue an activity as long as one or more children are interested. For more information on using this curriculum, see "Why Use Curriculum?" on page 8.

## Measuring with Blocks

**Collect**

Large cardboard blocks

**Do**

Help children stack blocks to their full height. Count the blocks.

**Say**

Justin, you are growing. Look how tall you are. God made you. He helps you grow taller.

Let's count the blocks that show how tall Justin is.

**Bonus Idea:** Show children how to stack blocks in different ways (horizontal, vertical, on sides).

## Crawl, Walk, Run

**Collect**

January Bible Story Picture from *I Love to Look!* or *Nursery Posters*

**Do**

Show and talk about Bible Story Picture.

In a large, open area of the room, lead children in crawling, walking, tiptoeing and jumping.

**Say**

Look at this picture of Jesus when He was a little boy. Once Jesus was a baby. Jesus learned to crawl. God helped Jesus to grow. Jesus learned to walk just like you learned.

Tyrell, you are growing! God is helping you grow.

Let's crawl like you did when you were a baby. Now let's walk and jump!

## Growing Up Tall

**Do**

Show children how to crouch low, and then stretch up tall.

**Say**

Marco, let's see how little you can be. Now let's see how tall you can be.

Reach up high! You are growing taller.

God helps you grow every day.

## Look What I Can Do!

**Collect**

Beanbag for each child and one for the teacher

**Do**

Model actions with your beanbag for children to imitate (walk with beanbag on shoulder, hold beanbag above head, etc.).

Ask interested children to try each action.

**Say**

I see Quinn is walking with the beanbag on her head. Quinn, you know how to do lots of things. God is helping you to grow.

Let's hold the beanbag way up high when we walk. Samantha, you can do it! God is helping you to grow!

We can thank God for helping you to grow and do new things.

## Body Tracing

**Collect**

January Bible Story Picture from *I Love to Look!* or *Nursery Posters*

3-foot (.9-m) length of butcher paper for each child

Marker

Crayons

**Do**

Before class, use marker to write "God helps me grow" at top of each length of butcher paper.

In class, show and talk about the Bible Story Picture.

Ask child to lie down on butcher paper, face up. Trace around child's body with crayon. Let children add to the drawing with crayons.

**Say**

Look at this picture to see what Jesus learned to do when He was a little boy. Jesus grew bigger and bigger just like you! He learned to do many things.

Jayce, look how big you are getting!

God helps you grow. Thank You, God, for helping Jayce to grow. Jesus grew just like you!

## Handprints

**Collect**

9x12-inch (23x30.5-cm) sheet of construction paper for each child

Marker

Crayons

**Do**

Before class, write "God helps me grow" at top of each paper.

In class, trace around each child's hands on his or her paper. Child colors on handprints.

**Say**

Look how big your hands are getting! Delaney, God loves you. God helps you grow.

We can thank God for helping you to grow and do new things with your hands.

## Food to Grow On

**Collect**

Large, plain white paper plates

Glue sticks

Pictures of healthy foods cut from magazines or grocery ads

**Do**

Children put glue on back of pictures and stick them to paper plate.

Talk about the foods children see.

**Say**

Jude, God gives you good food to help you grow. God loves you, Jude.

When we eat good food, our bodies grow. I'm glad God helps us grow.

## Texture Walk and Crawl

**Collect**

Approximately 1-foot (.3-m) square pieces of materials with different textures such as carpet square, bubble wrap, towel, fake fur fabric, floor tile

**Do**

Place materials on floor.

Invite children to remove their shoes and walk across the materials. Then have children crawl across.

**Say**

What does the fur feel like? It's soft, isn't it?

Leticia, you can walk or crawl. Can babies walk? No, they can't. You crawled when you were a baby, but now you can walk!

God helps you grow so that you can walk and run.

Bonus Idea: Cut materials into 3-inch (7.5-cm) squares, making two of each material. Put squares in bag. Children take turns removing squares and then matching them.

## Babies Grow

**Collect**

January Bible Story Picture from *I Love to Look!* or *Nursery Posters*

Sturdy picture books of babies and toddlers at different ages

**Do**

Show pictures to children.

Talk about differences between babies and toddlers.

**Say**

Annissa, when you were a baby, you couldn't walk, but now you are bigger.

God helps you grow. Once Jesus was a baby. When Jesus was a baby, He grew. Jesus learned to crawl. Then He learned to walk. Jesus grew to be a bigger boy—just like you.

## Measuring Growth

**Collect**

Marker

Measuring tape or stick

Length of butcher paper 4 feet (1.2-m) long

Painter's tape

**Do**

Before class, mark off inches (cm) from 1 to 48 (2.5 to 54) on the paper, using measuring tape or stick. Tape paper strip to a wall.

In class, ask children to stand next to wall and mark their height on the paper.

**Say**

Adriana, you are growing! See how tall you are?

God helps you grow.

When you were a baby, you were much smaller. Now you are growing taller! Thank You, God, for helping Adriana grow.

**Bonus Idea:** Provide a scale for children to stand on to measure weight.

## Heavy or Light?

**Collect**

Toys

Several canned foods

**Do**

Set out several toys and cans of food in a row.

Ask a child to pick up each one, and pick up an item yourself. Talk about whether the items are heavy or light.

**Say**

Look how strong you are, Laura. God loves you. He helps you grow.

Nathan, you are growing so big! God planned for you to grow. God made you! You are getting stronger every day.

## Plants Grow and So Do I

**Collect**

Sweet potato

Four toothpicks

Clear container a little wider than the sweet potato

**Do**

Before class, poke toothpicks ½-inch (1.3-cm) into the center of the sweet potato. Suspend the sweet potato over the container, using the toothpicks. Fill the container with water until the bottom third of the sweet potato is immersed in water.

In class, set the container on a table where children can see it. Check each week for plant growth.

**Say**

Our potato plant is growing, just like you are. God helps plants grow. He helps you grow, too. God made you. God loves you!

## Marching

**Collect**

*I Love to Sing!* CD (or other recorded music with a marching beat) and player

**Do**

Play "Grow Song" or other music.
Lead children in marching around the room.

**Say**

Can you march with me? You are growing and learning how to march.
God helps you grow. God planned for your legs to grow strong so you can march.

## Are You Sleeping?

**Collect**

*I Love to Sing!* CD (or other recorded lullabies) and player
Large blanket

**Do**

Spread blanket on floor.
Play "Blessing," "Twinkling Stars" or other lullaby.
Have children pretend to sleep when music is playing.
Stop music briefly every 20 seconds or so.
Children "wake up" when music stops and go back to "sleep" when it starts again. Continue as long as children are interested.

**Say**

God planned for us to sleep sometimes. Sleeping helps our bodies to grow and be healthy.
God made you. God helps you to grow. Thank You, God, for helping us to grow.

## This Is the Way

**Do**

Sing the following words to the tune of "Mulberry Bush," demonstrating the actions as you sing about them:

This is the way I eat my food,
eat my food, eat my food.
This is the way I eat my food.
God helps me to grow. (*Stretch up tall.*)

This is the way I run and play,
run and play, run and play.
This is the way I run and play.
God helps me to grow. (*Stretch up tall.*)

This is the way I go to sleep,
go to sleep, go to sleep.
This the way I go to sleep.
God helps me to grow. (*Stretch up tall.*)

**Say**

Juan, God helps you grow by giving you good food to eat. Let's sing about the ways God helps you grow.
Jesus grew and grew—just like you are!
**Bonus Idea:** Ask children to name a food he or she likes to eat. Use name of food in the song.

## God Helps Me Grow

**Collect**

January Bible Story Picture from *I Love to Look!* or *Nursery Posters*

**Do**

Show and talk about the Bible Story Picture.
Sing the following words, to the tune of "Mary Had a Little Lamb" at appropriate moments while children are playing with balls, ride-on toys, etc.

I am growing big and tall,
big and tall, big and tall.
I am growing big and tall.
God helps me to grow.

**Say**

Sarah, Jesus grew and learned to walk and play just like you! In this picture, Jesus is learning how to walk. Jesus learned to do many things as He grew.
God helps you grow. Let's sing about how you are growing bigger and taller.
Thank You, God, for helping Sarah grow.

## Birthday Party

**Collect**
Party hats
Birthday themed paper plates and napkins
Toy food

**Do**
Children pretend to be at a birthday party, setting out plates, napkins and toy food. Children may enjoy wearing party hats.
Participate in the party yourself. Sing "Happy Birthday" to each child.

**Say**
Have you ever been to a birthday party? What did you do? What did you eat?
Let's pretend it's Krystal's birthday. Krystal, how old are you now? God is helping you grow.
Brendan, you are growing. God made you. God helps you grow.

## Going to the Doctor

**Collect**
Dolls
Doll blankets
Optional—white shirts, doctor kit

**Do**
Children pretend to wrap their babies in blankets and take them to the doctor.
You can be the doctor who pretends to weigh and measure the babies. (Optional: Children wear white shirts and use doctor kit to pretend to be doctors.)

**Say**
Let's take our babies to the doctor. The doctor checks our babies to see if they are growing.
Isaac, your mom or dad takes you to the doctor. You are growing, too.
God helps you grow. God helps us all grow.
**Bonus Idea:** Let child use a stroller to bring baby to the doctor.

## Feeding My Baby

**Collect**
January Bible Story Picture from *I Love to Look!* or *Nursery Posters*
Baby dolls
Several small plastic bowls
Several spoons

**Do**
Show and talk about the Bible Story Picture. Children pretend to feed their "babies."

**Say**
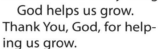
Jesus grew big and strong. Jesus grew and grew and grew! Look at this picture of Jesus. He is learning to walk. Jesus learned to do many things.
God helps us grow. Thank You, God, for helping us grow.
Darnell, when you were a baby your mom and dad took good care of you. They fed you good food. You grew big and strong!

## Grownup Time

**Collect**
Several empty purses and/or lightweight briefcases

**Do**
Set out purses and/or briefcases. Let interested children open and shut them. Children may also enjoy putting toys into and out of the purses and/or briefcases.

**Say**
Fernando, you are carrying the briefcase. Some day you will be all grown up. You might take a briefcase to your work.
God is helping you grow. God made you.

## Magazine Puzzles

**Collect**

Laminated pictures of babies and toddlers cut from magazines, reflecting the diversity of the children in your class (optional—cover pictures with clear Con-Tact paper)

Scissors

**Do**

Before class, cut some pictures into two pieces, some into three and some into four.

In class, show children the assembled pictures.

Take one apart and see if children can reassemble it.

Talk about the children in the pictures.

**Say**

Is this a baby or a big girl?

Julie, you are getting to be a big girl, aren't you? God made you.

God helps you grow. God helped Jesus grow, too.

## Drawing

**Collect**

Drawing paper
Jumbo crayons

**Do**

Give children paper and crayons.

Let children draw freely.

**Say**

I see Elise is drawing red lines. You know how to use crayons. You are growing.

God helps you grow. God helps you learn to do new things.

We can thank God for helping you to grow and grow and grow!

**Bonus Idea:** Provide varieties of paper for children to use (wallpaper samples, card stock, aluminum foil, etc.).

## Who Is It For?

**Collect**

Baby items (rattle, baby bottle, small sleeper, teething toy, etc.)

Toddler items (sippy cup, spoon, ball, etc.)

Bag

**Do**

Before class, put baby and toddler items in a bag.

In class, bring items out of bag, one at a time. Help child tell if the items are used by a baby or an older child.

**Say**

Who is this for? A baby or a big girl or boy?

Sienna, you were a baby. Now you are a bigger girl.

God helps you grow. Thank You, God, for helping us to grow.

## Growing Up Books

**Collect**

January Bible Story Picture from *I Love to Look!* or *Nursery Posters*

Several sturdy picture books that show activities children enjoy (indoor or outdoor play, playing with friends, etc.)

**Do**

Look at books with children and talk about the pictures. If children are interested, read the text.

**Say**

Olivia, when you were a baby, you crawled on the floor. Now you can walk. You are growing.

Jesus was a baby, too. His family took good care of Him. Jesus learned to crawl. Then Jesus learned to walk. God helped Him grow. God helps you to grow.

# February

## My Family Loves Me

### Timothy Learned About God's Love
(See 2 Timothy 1:5; 3:15.)

### "God gives us families."
(See Psalm 68:6.)

**This month you will help each child:**

• hear words and songs about God's gift of families;

• feel appreciation for his or her family members;

• identify family members and demonstrate ways they love him or her.

## Devotional

Three short verses about Timothy's early years tantalize us. Read Acts 16:1; 2 Timothy 1:5; 3:15. There is so much more we would like to know. How did his mother and grandmother go about teaching him the Scriptures? At what age did they begin their instruction? In what ways did Lois and Eunice share their faith with Timothy? How did they overcome the difficulty of Timothy's father probably being an unbeliever?

All we see are the results. Perhaps it is best that Paul did not share Eunice's child-raising "secrets." Every parent since would have felt compelled to follow the same exact procedures, possibly losing sight of the one crucial fact that the apostle Paul shares in this letter to Timothy, now an adult. Paul tells us that both Lois and Eunice possessed a sincere faith. Their task was to help make this faith meaningful to young Timothy. Because Christ dwelt within them, it was natural for His love to flow through them to Timothy. There must have been times of struggle and disappointment for Lois and Eunice, but sincere faith in Christ gave them a steady foundation.

As you seek to minister to young children, first make sure that Jesus is your Savior and Lord. Then your ministry to little ones will be based in the sincerity of personal experience.

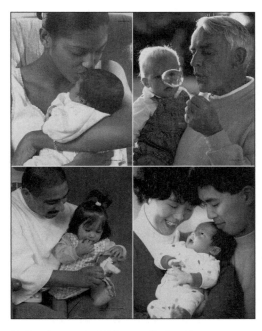

During the month of February, display this poster at child's eye level. Talk about the way in which family members are showing love to their children.

## Do It!

### Families

We all live in families,
You and me.
What kinds of families?
Let me see!
Tall ones and short ones;
Big ones and small ones.
We all live in families,
You and me.

## Sing It!

### My Family

(Tune: "Row, Row, Row Your Boat")

Thank, thank, thank You, God
For my family!
God made families to love
And care for you and me!

## Tell It!

### Timothy Learned About God's Love

Timothy was a little child, just like you.
Timothy liked good things to eat,
And he liked to play, just like you.
Timothy's mommy and grandma loved God.
They taught him about God.
Timothy learned that God
loves boys and girls
And grown-ups, too.
Timothy learned to love God, just like you.
(See 2 Timothy 1:5; 3:15.)

Display this poster at teacher's eye level in your nursery. Tell the Bible story, sing the song, do the finger play and repeat the Bible verse to one or more interested children.

## Activities with Children

Choose one or more of the learning activities on pages 51-56 to provide for children during a session. Consider your facility, the number of children and teachers and the supplies you have available as you plan which activities you will use. The best kind of teaching for toddlers will happen as you take advantage of teachable moments as children play and experience the learning activities you have provided. Continue an activity as long as one or more children are interested. For more information on using this curriculum, see "Why Use Curriculum?" on page 8.

## Red Light, Green Light

**Collect**

Red and green construction paper
Ruler
Scissors
Glue
Large craft stick

**Do**

Before class, cut two 8-inch (20.5-cm) circles—one red and one green. Glue the circles together with the craft stick in between for a handle.

In class, ask the children if they would like to pretend to drive a car. Show them how to pretend to steer the car while walking.

Guide them to "go" when you hold up the "green light" and "stop" when you hold up the "red light."

**Bonus Idea:** Children use ride-on toys.

**Say**

Jackson, where does your family like to go in the car? Let's pretend to go to the park. Uh, oh, the light is turning red, so we need to stop.

Your family keeps you safe in the car.

Your family loves you. Thank You, God, for Jackson's dad and grandma.

## Balls

**Collect**

Several large, soft balls

**Do**

Children roll and throw the balls.

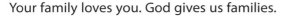

**Say**

Kaylie, do you have a ball at home? Who plays ball with you?

Families have fun together.

Your family loves you. God gives us families.

## Build a House

**Collect**

February Bible Story Picture from *I Love to Look!* or *Nursery Posters*
Large cardboard blocks
Toy people (too large to choke on) representing a variety of family members

**Do**

Show and talk about the Bible Story Picture. Encourage children to help you build a house with the blocks. Children play with toy people, pretending they are family members.

**Say**

Where is the boy in this picture? His name is Timothy. Timothy was a little child, just like you. The Bible tells us that his mom and grandma loved him. They told him about God's love.

God gave you a mommy to love you.

Schyler, you're holding the daddy for this family. God gave you a daddy to love you. Moms and dads can tell us about God's love.

## Follow the Road

**Collect**

Toy cars (no small parts)
Painter's or masking tape

**Do**

Create a road on the floor with the tape. (Remove tape after use.)

Children "drive" the cars along the road.

**Say**

I'm driving to the store to buy some food for my family.

God gave you a family to take care of you. Your family loves you.

**Bonus Idea:** Children use ride-on toys to follow the road.

## Washing Dishes

**Collect**
One or two dishpans
Toy dishes
Dish towels

**Do**
Children pretend to wash and dry dishes.

**Say**
Who washes the dishes at your house? Your big sister wants you to have clean dishes to eat from.
Your family loves you. God gives us families because He loves us.
Thank You, God, for our sisters and brothers and moms and dads.

## "My Family Loves Me" Picture

**Collect**
February Bible Story Picture from *I Love to Look!* or *Nursery Posters*
Construction paper
Marker
Crayons

**Do**
Before class, print the words, "My Family Loves Me" near the top of each paper. Draw two or more happy faces on each paper, representing each child's family members.

In class, show and talk about the Bible Story Picture. Children color faces. Talk about each child's family members and how they love the child.

**Say**
Here is a picture of a family. The Bible tells us about this family. There is a boy named Timothy, a mom and a grandma. Timothy's family loved him. Timothy learned that God loves boys and girls.
I see there are three people in your family, Henry. Your family loves you. God gave you a family because He loves you.

## Valentines

**Collect**
Red, white, and pink construction paper
Scissors
Ruler
Valentine stickers
Crayons

**Do**
Before class, cut heart shapes at least 6 inches (15 cm) in size out of construction paper.
In class, invite one or two children at a time to make a valentine. Children decorate valentines with stickers and crayons.

**Say**
We give valentines to the people we love. Who would you like to give your valentine to?
God gave you a family to love you. Your family takes good care of you.

## Play Dough Hearts

**Note:** This activity is best used with children over the age of two.

**Collect**
Commercial or freshly-made non-toxic play dough
Fabric sheet or tarp
Masking tape
Heart-shaped cookie cutters
Small rolling pins or 6-inch (15-cm) lengths of 1-inch (2.5-cm) dowels

**Do**
Before class, tape sheet or tarp to floor under a child-sized table.
Help children roll out the dough. Carefully watch to be sure that children do not eat dough.
Children use the cookie cutters to make heart shapes.

**Say**
My family loves me. A heart reminds me of love. I'm glad my family loves me.
Annie, your family loves you, too. God gives us families because He loves us.
**Bonus Idea:** Help children form play dough birthday cakes. Children place candles in dough.

## Listen to Your Heart

**Collect**
Bandages
Dolls

**Do**
Children take care of "hurt" dolls by putting bandages on them (and themselves, if interested).

**Say**
Who helps you when you are hurt? Who puts a bandage on you?

Annissa, your mom and dad take care of you because they love you.

I'm thankful that God gives us families! Families help take care of us.

**Bonus Idea:** Provide one or more real or play stethoscopes. Invite children to listen or pretend to listen to their own heartbeat.

## Your Family Loves You

**Collect**
February Bible Story Picture from *I Love to Look!* or *Nursery Posters*
Unbreakable mirror

**Do**
Show and talk about the Bible Story Picture.
Show a child his or her reflection in the mirror.

**Say**
Lauren, look at the boy in this picture. His mommy and grandma love him. They take good care of him. The Bible tells us that this boy's name was Timothy. Timothy's mommy and grandma loved God. They taught him about God.

Who does your family love? That's right . . . you! God made mommies and daddies. Your mommy and daddy love you. They take good care of you.

Let's tell God thank You for giving us families. Thank You, God, for our families.

## House Plants

**Collect**
One or more non-poisonous houseplants
Water
Small watering can

**Do**
Invite children to help water plants. (Optional: Children water plants in enclosed play yard.)

**Say**
Paloma, do you have plants at home? Who takes care of them?

Your family takes care of you, too.

Your family loves you. God made your family to care for you. God gives us families because He loves us.

## Toast for Breakfast

**Note:** Post a note alerting parents to the use of food. Also, check children's registration forms for possible food allergies.

**Collect**
Bread slices
Toaster
Plastic knife
Butter
Paper plates and napkins

**Do**
Set up toaster where children are unable to reach it. Toast a slice of bread. Spread butter on toast, cut in half and serve each half to an interested child.

**Say**
Calvin, who makes breakfast at your house? What do you like to eat for breakfast?

Your family cooks good food for you to eat.

Your family loves you. God planned for you to have a family that loves you.

## Song: My Family Loves Me So

### Collect
Photo of each child's family or a construction paper heart shape
Large craft sticks
Craft glue

### Do
Before class, glue craft stick to back of photo or heart shape to create a handle.

In class, give each child his or her family photo or heart shape to hold.

Sing the following song to the tune of "The Farmer in the Dell":

My family loves me so. My family loves me so.
God gave me a family. My family loves me so.

Continue singing, replacing "family" with names of other family members.

### Say
Brianna, you are holding a heart. Hearts remind us of the people who love us.

God planned for families to love us and care for us.

## Valentine Shakers

### Collect
*I Love to Sing!* CD and player
Heart-shaped boxes from craft store
Unpopped popcorn
Large spoon
Strong glue or tape
Stickers

### Do
Before class, place a spoonful unpopped corn into a box. Glue or tape lid on securely.

In class, give each child a box. Children place stickers on boxes for decoration.

Encourage children to shake their boxes while listening to "My Family Cares".

### Say
Let's listen to a song about our families. God gives us families to love us.

Thank You, God, for Savannah's family.

## The Wheels on the Car

### Collect
Four or more chairs

### Do
Place chairs together to resemble a car. Invite children to go for a "ride." Sing the following words to the tune of "The Wheels on the Bus":

The wheels on the car go round and round, round and round, round and round.
The wheels on the car go round and round all through the town.

Repeat song, singing, "The parents in the car say, 'I love you.'" and "The children in the car say, 'I love you.'"

### Say
Where is this family going? They are going to the park. Families have fun at the park.

God gives us families to play with. We love our families.

**Bonus Idea:** Children place dolls on chairs to go for a "ride."

## Ribbon Dancing

### Collect
February Bible Story Picture from *I Love to Look!* or *Nursery Posters*
*I Love to Sing!* CD and player
18-inch (45.5-cm) lengths of ribbon, two for each child and teacher

### Do
Show and talk about the Bible Story Picture.

Play "Happy Family." Give children a ribbon to hold in each hand. Children "dance" in time to the music and wave ribbons.

### Say
Look at the family in this picture. They love each other. They are happy. The Bible tells us about this boy. His name is Timothy. His mom and grandma told him about God's love.

We can wave these ribbons to show that we are happy. We're happy because our families love us. I'm happy your family loves you.

## Time for Bed

**Collect**

Several pillows and blankets

Storybooks

**Do**

Guide children to arrange pillows and blankets to make "beds."

Look at books with children before children go to bed.

**Say**

Let's pretend it's bedtime. Bailey, here is a blanket and pillow for you.

Jacqueline, would you like me to read you a story? Who helps you get ready for bed?

Your family loves you. Your mom and dad take good care of you. God gives us families.

## Family Walk

**Collect**

February Bible Story Picture from *I Love to Look!* or *Nursery Posters*

Masking tape

Toy people

**Do**

Before class, make several roads on the floor with masking tape.

In class, show and talk about the Bible Story Picture. Children pretend toy people are families "walking" on the roads.

**Say**

How many people are in the picture of this family? The boy's name is Timothy. The Bible tells us that his mom and grandma told him about God's love. They took good care of him.

Your family loves you. They take care of you.

I see a mom and little boy walking on the road. Where is your family going?

## Making Breakfast

**Collect**

Toy dishes and food

Clean and empty cereal boxes and milk cartons

**Do**

Children pretend to make and eat breakfast.

**Say**

Let's pretend to make some breakfast.

Benjamin, what did you have for breakfast today? Who made your breakfast?

Your family loves you. I'm glad God gives you a grandpa to make pancakes for breakfast.

**Bonus Idea:** Give children small bowls of dry cereal to eat. (Post a note alerting parents to the use of food. Also, check children's registration forms for possible food allergies.)

## Going to Grandma's

**Collect**

Small suitcases, backpacks and/or tote bags

Books

Toys

**Do**

Children pack items in suitcases, backpacks or tote bags. Guide children to walk to another part of the room, pretending they are going to visit a grandparent. Children unpack items.

**Say**

Let's pretend we are going to Grandma's house. What shall we put in our suitcase?

Cyndi, do you have a grandma or grandpa? Do you go to their house?

It's fun to be with our families. God gives us families to love us. Thank You, God, for our families.

## Doll House

**Collect**

Sturdy doll house with toy furniture and toy people (optional—cardboard box or large shoe box)

**Do**

Place doll house on a child-sized table. (Optional: Turn box on its side to represent a house.)

Invite up to two children to play with it at once.

**Say**

Mariana, I see that you are holding the mommy. What is she doing?

Who cooks breakfast at your house? What else does your mom do?

I'm glad God gave you a family to love you.

**Bonus Idea:** Give children small fabric squares to use in their doll house play.

## Heart Match

**Collect**

February Bible Story Picture from *I Love to Look!* or *Nursery Posters*

Craft foam sheets or felt in various colors

Scissors

**Do**

Before class, cut a pair of identical hearts from each color of foam or felt.

In class, show and talk about the Bible Story Picture.

Invite one child at a time to find two hearts that match. Tell (or ask) the color of each pair as they are matched.

**Say**

Brent, here is a pink heart. Can you find another pink heart? Hearts make me think of love.

Your family loves you very much. God gave you a family to love you.

The Bible tells us about a boy named Timothy and his family. Timothy's mom and grandma told him about God. Can you point to Timothy in the picture?

## Bedtime Stories

**Collect**

Several sturdy picture books about families

Sturdy Bible storybook

**Do**

Read one or more stories to interested children, and/or look at pictures with children.

**Say**

Jessie, who reads stories to you at home? What else does your dad do with you? I'm glad you have a dad who loves you.

God gave you a family to love you.

Thank You, God, for Jessie's family.

## What's for Dinner?

**Collect**

Laminated pictures of food cut from magazines or grocery ads (optional—cover with clear Con-Tact paper if laminator is not available)

Large, sturdy paper plates

**Do**

Give each child a paper plate.

Set out foods on table or floor and identify them.

Children choose foods they like to eat and place them on their plates.

**Say**

Look at these pictures of food. Which food do you like to eat? Who cooks it for you?

Your family loves you and gives you good food to eat.

God planned for you to have a family to take good care of you.

# March

## Jesus Loves Me

### Jesus Loved Zacchaeus
(See Luke 19:1-6.)

### "Jesus loves us."
(See Revelation 1:5.)

· · · · · · · · · · · ·

### This month you will help each child:

• hear words and songs about Jesus' love;

• feel glad to hear of Jesus' love and to be cared for by loving teachers;

• participate in play activities to learn about Jesus' love.

## Devotional

Zacchaeus was a hated man. He boldly enriched himself at the expense of others, hiding behind the authority of the Roman government, hurting people right and left. His behavior was a lot like what we might see in a cranky toddler—grabby, aggressive, unable to focus on anyone but himself.

While Zacchaeus's focus on "ME" and "MINE!" was a normal response when he (himself) was only a toddler, he seems to have never grown beyond it to treat other people with compassion. Instead, he became an adult who was just plain selfish and cruel. Do you suppose he was treated cruelly as a little one, teaching him that cruelty was acceptable when one got big enough or powerful enough to bully other people? Did he live with selfishness that taught him it was the way to live? Although it's true that children learn what they live with, it may have been none of those factors. But whatever the cause may have been, the only cure for his childish attitude was Jesus' love!

You may feel like there's a child or two in your nursery with real "Zacchaeus potential"! But remember that it is Jesus' love that changes people—no matter what their age or height or problem. And Jesus' love can flow through you as you sing, play, feed and teach these little ones who learn what they live. Take time before you enter the nursery to ask Him to give you His love to share. He loves to answer such prayers! And recognize that as you treat these little ones with love—the kind of love God has shown you in Jesus—you are teaching powerful lessons, lessons that may help your toddlers outgrow the "Zacchaeus Syndrome"!

During the month of March, display this poster at child's eye level. Talk about Jesus' love for children and the way in which the dad in the poster is showing love and care for his child.

## Do It!

### Day and Night

When the sun is in the sky,
Jesus loves me.
When the stars are way up high,
Jesus loves me.
In the day and in the night,
While I play and then sleep tight,
Jesus loves me.

## Sing It!

### Yes, Jesus Loves You

(Tune: Refrain to "Jesus Loves Me")

Yes, Jesus loves you.
Yes, Jesus loves you.
Yes, Jesus loves you!
The Bible tells us so.

## Tell It!

### Jesus Loved Zacchaeus

Zacchaeus wanted to see Jesus.
But Zacchaeus was little.
Zacchaeus couldn't see
over the taller people.
So he climbed up into a tree!
Now he could see Jesus.
Jesus saw Zacchaeus, too.
Jesus loved Zacchaeus.
And Jesus loves you!
(See Luke 19:1-6.)

Display this poster at teacher's eye level in your nursery. Tell the Bible story, sing the song, do the finger play and repeat the Bible verse to one or more interested children.

## Activities with Children

Choose one or more of the learning activities on pages 59-64 to provide for children during a session. Consider your facility, the number of children and teachers and the supplies you have available as you plan which activities you will use. The best kind of teaching for toddlers will happen as you take advantage of teachable moments as children play and experience the learning activities you have provided. Continue an activity as long as one or more children are interested. For more information on using this curriculum, see "Why Use Curriculum?" on page 8.

## Climb the Tree

**Collect**

March Bible Story Picture from *I Love to Look!* or *Nursery Posters*
Green construction paper
Scissors
Masking tape

**Do**

Before class, cut large leaf shapes out of construction paper.

In class, show and talk about the Bible Story Picture.

Let children tape leaves to walls or furniture in the room.

**Say**

This is a picture of Zacchaeus and Jesus. Zacchaeus climbed a tree so that he could see Jesus. Jesus loved Zacchaeus. Jesus loves you, too.

Here is a leaf, Benjamin. Leaves grow on trees. Where do you want to put your leaf?

## Zacchaeus Climbed the Tree

**Collect**

Small artificial tree branch
Toy people (too large to swallow)

**Do**

Hold the branch like a tree and move the toy people to briefly tell the story of Zacchaeus.

Show children how to make the people climb the tree.

Children play with branch and people.

**Say**

This girl wants to climb the tree, like Zacchaeus did. Here she goes: up, up, up.

Jesus said, "Come down, Zacchaeus. I want to go to your house."

Jesus loved Zacchaeus. He loves you, too.

## Everywhere I Go

**Collect**

Toys that represent different locations (house, garage, cars, farm, etc.)
Toy people (too large to swallow)

**Do**

Arrange location toys several feet from each other. Children move people from place to place.

**Say**

Let's pretend we're going to the farm. Let's move our people to the farm. Jesus loves us when we're at a farm. Jesus loves us everywhere we go.

Jonah, you put the little boy in the car. Jesus loves you when you are riding in the car. Jesus loves you everywhere you go.

Thank You, Jesus, for loving us.

## Where Are the People Jesus Loves?

**Collect**

Toy people (too large to swallow)

**Do**

Put toy people around the room in places easily seen by children. Walk with interested children around the room to find the people.

**Say**

Jesus loves each person. Let's see if we can find some people. Natalie, you found a little girl! Jesus loves little girls. Jesus loves little boys, too.

Brendan, who did you find? Jesus loves daddies. Jesus loves mommies, too.

I'm glad Jesus loves us.

**Bonus Idea:** Give children a clean, large plastic jar with lid to put people into and out of.

## Photo Frame

**Collect**

Photo of each child

White cardboard cut 1-inch (2.5-cm) larger than photo on all sides, one for each child

Marker

Heart-shaped rubber stamps

Washable red ink pad

Glue

**Do**

Print the words "Jesus Loves Me" at the top of each frame.

Help child attach photo to frame with glue.

Child decorates frame with stamps.

**Say**

These words say, "Jesus Loves Me."

Who is in this picture? Jesus loves YOU, Vanessa.

Jesus loves each person in our class. Thank You, Jesus, for loving us.

## Leaf Collage

**Collect**

March Bible Story Picture from *I Love to Look!* or *Nursery Posters*

Green construction paper cut into leaf shapes (optional—real leaves)

Large paper plates

Glue sticks (optional—white glue)

**Do**

Show and talk about the Bible Story Picture.

Help one child at a time spread glue onto a paper plate. Encourage child to glue leaves on plate any way he or she wishes. (Optional: Children look at and touch real leaves. Talk about the similarities and differences. Children use white glue to attach leaves to plates.)

**Say**

Look at this picture of a tree. The Bible tells us about a man named Zacchaeus. Zacchaeus climbed a tree to see Jesus.

Jesus loved Zacchaeus. Jesus loves you, too!

Leaves grow on trees. You can glue some leaves onto this plate.

## Drawing to Music

**Collect**

*I Love to Sing!* CD (or other recorded music about Jesus) and player

Drawing paper

Jumbo crayons

**Do**

Play "Jesus Loves Me."

Children draw on paper while listening to music.

Sing along with songs as you become familiar with them.

**Say**

This song is about Jesus. I like to sing about Jesus!

Jesus loves children and Jesus loves you!

## My Own Handprint

**Collect**

9x12-inch (23x30.5-cm) sheet of white construction paper for each child.

Jumbo crayons

Stickers

**Do**

Draw around each child's hand on a separate sheet of paper.

Print "Jesus Loves (child's name)" on each paper.

Children color hands and add stickers as decorations.

**Bonus Idea:** Help children remove socks and shoes. Trace around each child's feet.

**Say**

Adriana, this is your hand. Jesus loves you. Jesus loves everyone!

## Tree Walk

**Collect**

*I Love to Look!* March Bible Story Picture Card
Bag or basket
Real or artificial leaves

**Do**

Briefly tell the story of Zacchaeus.
Encourage children to touch and explore the leaves.
Children put leaves into and out of the bag or basket

**Say**

Jolie, you are picking up the leaves in our room. Leaves grow on trees.
The Bible tells us about a man named Zacchaeus. Zacchaeus climbed a tree so that he could see Jesus.
Jesus loved Zacchaeus. Jesus loves you. Thank You, Jesus, for Your love.
**Bonus Idea:** If weather permits, sit on a blanket by a tree in an enclosed play area and read the story of Zacchaeus.

## Texture Play

**Collect**

Variety of items that feel different (hard block, soft pillow, smooth fabric, feather, tissue paper, etc.)

**Do**

Children touch, play with and arrange the items you collected. Talk about how each item feels.

**Say**

Kelsey, you are touching the soft pillow.
We're having fun touching all these things. I'm glad to see you today. I love you, and Jesus loves you, too!
I'm glad that Jesus loves us.

## Colors All Around

**Collect**

Variety of toys with different colors

**Do**

As children play with toys, talk about the colors of the toys.

**Say**

James, you are playing with the red ball.
Your eyes can see so many colors. Jesus loves you.
Who sees something blue? Michael, you are playing with the blue truck. Jesus loves you, Michael.

## What's That Sound?

**Collect**

Toys and/or rhythm instruments that make sounds

**Do**

Set out the toys and/or rhythm instruments for children to explore. Describe the sounds that each toy or instrument makes.
Repeat the words "Jesus loves you" as you play an instrument.

**Say**

Listen to the sound this bell makes. Can you hear it? It's a loud bell.
Kelsey, you are playing the shaker. It's a soft sound.
Jesus loves you!

## Jesus Loves Me

**Do**

Sing the refrain of "Jesus Loves Me" at teachable moments (while playing with a child, while looking at a picture of Jesus, while going for a walk, etc.):

Yes, Jesus loves me.
Yes, Jesus loves me.
Yes, Jesus loves me.
The Bible tells me so.

**Bonus Idea:** Substitute child's name for the word "me" in the song.

**Say**

I'm glad Jesus loves me! He loves you, too! Let's sing about Jesus' love for us.

## Rhythm Sticks

**Collect**

*I Love to Sing!* CD (or other recorded music about Jesus' love) and player
Pair of rhythm sticks (or other rhythm instrument) for each child

**Do**

Play "Jesus Loves Me" or other music. Give each child a set of sticks. Show children how to tap rhythm sticks together safely.
Play music and demonstrate starting and stopping when the music starts and stops. Periodically stop the music and remind children to stop tapping sticks together.

**Say**

This song is about Jesus. Jesus loves us.
Jesus loves us at church. Jesus loves us when we are at home, too. Jesus always loves us.

## Let's Pretend

**Collect**

*I Love to Sing!* CD (or recording of light classical music) and player

**Do**

Play "A Happy Place" or other music and invite children to pretend to swim, fly like a bird, jump like a frog, etc.

**Say**

Let's pretend we're swimming in the water.
We're having fun at church today. At church we learn that Jesus loves us.
Jesus loves everyone. Jesus loves (name each child).

## Clapping Jesus' Love

**Collect**

March Bible Story Picture from *I Love to Look!* or *Nursery Posters*
*I Love to Sing!* CD (or other recorded music that tells about Jesus' love)

**Do**

Show and talk about the Bible Story Picture.
Play "Jesus Loves Us All." Invite children to clap with the music.

**Say**

The Bible tells us about a man named Zacchaeus. This picture shows us how he climbed a tree to see Jesus. Jesus loved Zacchaeus.
Jesus loves us! I'm glad Jesus loves us.
Let's sing a song about Jesus.
Can you clap like this?

## Friends for Dinner

**Collect**

Toy dishes and food

**Do**

Help children set the table, serve food and pretend to eat dinner with friends.

**Say**

Maria, who eats dinner at your house? Do friends come sometimes?

Jesus went to His friend Zacchaeus's house. Jesus loved Zacchaeus. Jesus loves you.

**Bonus Idea:** Serve crackers to children to eat together. (Post a note alerting parents to the use of food. Also, check children's registration forms for possible food allergies.)

## Picnic and Story

**Note:** Post a note alerting parents to the use of food. Also, check children's registration forms for possible food allergies.

**Collect**

March Bible Story Picture from *I Love to Look!* or sturdy picture books about Jesus

Picnic basket or large paper grocery bag

Blanket

Snack food and napkins

**Do**

Ask children if they would like to have a picnic. Let them help you pack the basket or bag.

Find a place indoors and spread out the blanket. Eat the snack food.

Read the story of Zacchaeus or other stories about Jesus.

**Say**

Jesus loved Zacchaeus.

And Jesus loves (name all of the children present).

Thank You, Jesus, for loving us.

## Jesus Loved Zacchaeus

**Collect**

March Bible Story Picture from *I Love to Look!* or *Nursery Posters*

One or more large scarves or large pieces of fabric

**Do**

Show and talk about the Bible Story Picture.

Let children pretend to be Zacchaeus by draping scarf or fabric over their shoulders or heads.

**Say**

Look at this picture of Zacchaeus. Zacchaeus was Jesus' friend. Zacchaeus wore clothes that are different from ours. Lily, do you want to pretend to be Zacchaeus? You can put this scarf over your shoulders.

Jesus loved Zacchaeus. Jesus loves you, too.

## People Puppets

**Collect**

Variety of people puppets

**Do**

Use a puppet to talk to a child.

Let interested children take turns using puppets. Be ready to help a child get a puppet on his or her hand.

**Say**

This is a little boy. He says, "Hello, Morgan. Jesus loves you."

Cara, which puppet do you want to play with? Let's use our puppets to say "Jesus loves me."

## I See Someone Jesus Loves

**Do**

Play a game like I Spy with children, describing each child in the group one at a time.

**Say**

I see someone Jesus loves. It's a girl wearing a red dress. Who is it? That's right! Jesus loves Kelly.

Let's find someone else Jesus loves. I see someone with trucks on his shirt. Who is it? That's right! Jesus loves Nick. I'm glad Jesus loves us.

## Who Loves You?

**Collect**

March Bible Story Picture from *I Love to Look!* or *Nursery Posters*

Shoe box with lid

Picture of Jesus that fits in the bottom of the box

Glue

**Do**

Before class, glue the picture to the bottom of the box.

In class, show and talk about the Bible Story Picture.

Show the box to one child at a time. Let children take turns opening the box.

**Say**

The Bible tells us about a man named Zacchaeus. He climbed a tree to see Jesus. Jesus loved Zacchaeus.

Let's see who loves you, Hailey. Can you open the box? It's the picture of Jesus! Jesus loves you, Hailey.

Tyler, look inside the box to find who loves you.

Jesus loves you! Jesus loves every one of us.

## Jesus Loves our Families

**Collect**

Sturdy books with pictures of families

**Do**

Look at the books with one or two children at a time.

Talk about the pictures.

Read the text if children are interested.

**Say**

Where's the daddy in this picture? There's the daddy. The daddy is holding his child. The daddy loves his child. Jesus loves you, too.

Let's count how many people are in this family. One, two, three, four. Jesus loves them all! Jesus loves you. Jesus loves the people in your family.

## Children Jesus Loves

**Collect**

Small photo of each child

Scissors

Lids from 12 oz. frozen juice containers

Strong glue

Large cookie sheet

1-inch (2.5-cm) strips of adhesive-backed magnets

**Do**

Before class, cut children's photos to fit inside juice can lids. Glue photos in place. Attach a magnet to the back of each lid.

In class, help children select and attach photos to cookie sheet or other magnetic surface.

**Say**

Let's find a picture of someone Jesus loves. Yes! Jesus loves Austin.

And Jesus loves you, Gabriel. Thank You, Jesus, for loving Austin and Gabriel.

**Bonus Idea:** Make enough magnets for each child to take one home.

# April

## God Makes Growing Things

### God Made the World
(See Genesis 1:11-31.)

### "God made everything."
(See Genesis 1:1.)

· · · · · · · · · · ·

**This month you will help each child:**

• hear words and songs about the world God made;

• feel awe at God's creation;

• participate in play activities to touch and see things God made.

## Devotional

And . . . it was good. These familiar words echo through the first chapter of Genesis. In springtime they seem to take on fresh luster as plants awaken from their long winter dormancy. There is something very good about new beginnings. Read Genesis 1:1-31.

Perhaps your spiritual life needs a new beginning, a reawakening from a period of seeming barrenness. Just as God's Spirit moved to bring beauty and order in the world's beginning, God Himself can bring light and life to the soul of anyone who is open to this love. God designed people in His own image to possess qualities that respond to His presence.

The good beginning for all creation came as God spoke. His Word still speaks today. Make time in your daily routines to read the Scriptures, asking God to help you respond.

Keep in mind that even the universe was not built in a day; six were needed to do the job! Expect God's work in your life to take place over a period of time as you gain spiritual insight according to His plan for you.

During the month of April, display this poster at child's eye level. Talk about the things that God made and the child's happiness in playing with the kittens.

## Do It!

### I'm a Little Seed

I'm a little, tiny seed
In the earth so low.
God sends sun and rain,
Then I start to grow.
Up, up, up,
Slowly I grow,
Then my leaves and flowers show!

## Sing It!

### Animal Friends

(Tune: "Jingle Bells" chorus)

Oh, God made ducks
And rabbits and squirrels
And little birds to sing.
God made you and God made me.
Yes, God made everything!
(Repeat.)

## Tell It!

### God Made the World

God made everything that grows.
He made green grass
And pretty flowers grow on the ground.
He made trees grow way up high.
God made puppies grow into dogs
And kittens grow into cats.
Little pigs grow into big pigs and
Little cows grow into big
cows that say "moo!"
God made little babies grow bigger
And bigger—just like you.
(See Genesis 1:11-31.)

Display this poster at teacher's eye level in your nursery. Tell the Bible story, sing the song, do the finger play and repeat the Bible verse to one or more interested children.

## Activities with Children

Choose one or more of the learning activities on pages 67-72 to provide for children during a session. Consider your facility, the number of children and teachers and the supplies you have available as you plan which activities you will use. The best kind of teaching for toddlers will happen as you take advantage of teachable moments as children play and experience the learning activities you have provided. Continue an activity as long as one or more children are interested. For more information on using this curriculum, see "Why Use Curriculum?" on page 8.

## Growing Seeds

**Collect**

Watering can
Some seeds in a small container

**Do**

Show children the seeds.
Show children how to crouch down to make themselves small like seeds.
Pretend to water them with watering can so they can "grow."

**Say**

These seeds are small. Isaiah, can you make yourself small like a seed?
When seeds get watered, they grow. When I water you with my watering can, you can pretend to be a seed and grow big!
God made seeds to grow into plants. God made everything that grows.

## Hide and Seek Animals

**Collect**

Several small stuffed animals

**Do**

Before class, hide stuffed toy animals around the room. Make sure part of each animal is visible.
In class, ask children to find the hidden animals and make the appropriate animal sounds.

**Say**

Laura, you found the dog! What sound does it make?
God made all the animals. God made animals to grow!
I'm glad God made dogs and cats and birds.
**Bonus Idea:** Use stuffed animals that make sounds and conceal them completely so children have to listen to find them.

## Animal Actions

**Collect**

April Bible Story Picture from *I Love to Look!* or *Nursery Posters*
Sturdy picture books of animals such as rabbit, snake, frog, and spider

**Do**

Look at the pictures with children. Show children how to move like each animal.
Ask interested children to try moving like each animal.

**Say**

God made everything that grows. God made all the animals. Look at the pictures of these animals.
Can you wiggle like a snake? Can you run like a puppy? Can you hop like a frog?

## Watering Plants

**Collect**

One or more small watering cans with small amount of water
Several indoor or outdoor plants

**Do**

Children use watering cans to water plants.

**Say**

God makes growing things.
Kobi, growing things need water. Would you like to give our plants a drink?
God made trees and plants that grow. Thank You, God, for trees and plants.

## Animal Pictures

**Collect**

April Bible Story Picture from *I Love to Look!* or *Nursery Posters*

Sheet of construction paper for each child

Animal stickers

**Do**

Show and talk about the Bible Story Picture.

Children attach stickers to their papers. Tell children the names of the animals.

Children make animal sounds.

**Say**

This picture shows a dog. Who has a pet dog at home?

God made puppies that grow into dogs. God made everything that grows.

Jodie, have you been to the zoo and seen an elephant? God made elephants. God made you!

## Bird Play

**Note:** Post a note alerting parents to the use of food. Also, check children's registration forms for possible food allergies.

**Collect**

Raisins

Paper plates

Several toy birds

Optional—birdseed, plastic tub, plastic tablecloth

**Do**

Place several raisins on each paper plate. (Optional: Place tub on tablecloth and put birdseed into tub. Children feel the seeds and use them in their pretend play.)

Children play with the birds, pretending that the birds are eating the "seeds."

**Say**

Let's pretend our birds are eating the seeds.

God made birds. God made seeds for birds to eat so they can grow.

God made red birds. God made yellow birds. God made black birds. God made all the birds!

## God Made Ducks

**Collect**

Large plastic tub filled part way with water

Large towel

Several small rubber ducks

**Do**

Place tub on towel.

Children float ducks in the water.

**Say**

Ducks can swim on top of the water like this. Let's make sounds like ducks.

God made ducks. Ducks grow, just like you are growing.

Thank You, God, for ducks.

## Animal Sounds

**Collect**

Pop-up animal toys and/or toys that make animal sounds

**Do**

Children play with toys.

Encourage children to name the animals they see on the toy. Children make animal sounds and/or imitate the animal sounds they hear.

**Say**

Caleb, what animal do you see? That's right—it's a pig. What sound does a pig make?

God made pigs. God made lots of animals that grow.

Zachary, you're having fun making animals sounds. God made all the animals!

## Nature Search

### Collect
Magazine pictures of nature items displayed on walls at children's eye level
One or more toy binoculars

### Do
Guide children to look through windows or around the room to see growing things such as people, trees, plants, flowers, insects and birds. (Optional: Take children on a walk in an enclosed play area.)

### Say
Look! Do you see the bird on the fence? God made all the birds.

I see lots of things that are growing in the picture on the wall. I see small trees and big trees. Trees grow. God made trees.

Seth, what do you see that God made? I'm glad God made everything.

## Long or Short?

### Collect
April Bible Story Picture from *I Love to Look!* or *Nursery Posters*
12-inch (30.5-cm) length of yarn or string for each child

### Do
Show and talk about the Bible Story Picture.

Let children use yarn or string to measure items in the room. Talk about whether the items are longer or shorter than the yarn or string.

### Say
Kylie, what animals do you see in this picture? Put your finger on the cow. God made all the animals! Animals need food and water to grow. God gives us what we need to grow.

Anthony, let's see if this car is longer or shorter than your string. It's shorter. Anthony, you are bigger than the string. You are growing! God is helping you to grow!

## Smell the Flowers

### Collect
One or more kinds of flowers
Unbreakable vase filled part way with water

### Do
Let children help you place flowers in vase. Invite children to see, smell and touch the flowers.

Place flowers out of reach when their use is not supervised.

### Say
Look at the beautiful flowers God made. He gives them rain and dirt to help them grow.

## Comparing Plants

### Collect
Several small (non-poisonous) potted plants (with different leaves, with and without flowers, etc.)

### Do
Place plants on a child-sized table where children can see them easily.

Talk about the similarities and differences.

### Say
William, look at this plant. It has pretty red flowers.

This plant has no flowers, but it has big shiny leaves.

God made lots of different plants. God makes growing things.

**Bonus Idea:** Keep one or more plants in the classroom indefinitely and let children help care for it.

## Seed Shakers

**Collect**

*I Love to Sing!* CD and player
Small, clear, plastic water bottle for each child
Any kind of seeds (bird, plant)
Duct tape

**Do**

Before class, place some seeds into the bottle. Securely tape the bottle shut.

In class, children use shakers as they listen and march to "God Made Grins."

**Say**

Cameron, do you see the seeds in your bottle? Flowers grow from seeds.

God made seeds. God made the flowers that grow. God made you, too. God planned for you to grow!

## Birds Are Flying

**Collect**

April Bible Story Picture from *I Love to Look!* or *Nursery Posters*
*I Love to Sing!* CD and player
Two small scarves for each child

**Do**

Show and talk about the Bible Story Picture.

Give each child two scarves for bird wings.

Play "Growing Things" on CD. Children wave scarves up and down to "fly like birds." Children may also move around the room as they "fly."

**Say**

Maggie, look at the animals in this picture. God made the cows. God made pigs. God made all the animals that grow.

God made birds that grow. God made birds with wings so they can fly. Annie, I see that you are "flying" like a bird.

The Bible tells us that God made everything that grows!

## Animal Movements

**Collect**

*I Love to Sing!* CD and player (optional—a recording of Camille Saint-Saens' *Carnival of the Animals*)

**Do**

Play "Growing Things." Invite children to move like the animals named in the song while the music plays. (Optional: Play selections from the *Carnival of the Animals*, such as "Elephants," "Tortoises," and "Kangaroos.")

**Say**

Let's walk like elephants. We see elephants at the zoo. God made those great big elephants.

God made all the animals. God made everything that grows!

God made you so that you are growing! Thank You, God!

## God Makes Growing Things

**Collect**

Sturdy picture books that show growing things

**Do**

Show pictures to children and identify them. As each picture is identified, sing the following words to the tune of "God Is So Good":

God made the dogs, God made the dogs, God made the dogs, God makes growing things.

**Say**

Kelsey, can you find the picture of the dog? God made dogs. God made everything that grows.

I'm glad that God made dogs and cats. I'm glad that God made birds and flowers. I'm glad that God made you!

God makes everything grow!

## Birds in a Nest

**Collect**

Sturdy book with picture(s) of birds in a nest (optional—real bird nest)

Wading pool or masking tape

Blankets and small pillows

**Do**

Before class, if wading pool is not available, use masking tape to outlne a circle on the floor for a "nest."

During class, show picture of bird nest to children and talk about it. (Optional: Show real bird nest.)

With children's help, place blankets inside pool to make a "bird nest."

Children pretend to be birds (make chirping sounds, flap wings, etc.) and play in the nest.

**Say**

God made birds. When birds are babies, they live in a nest. God helps baby birds grow bigger and bigger. God is helping you grow bigger and bigger, too.

Let's pretend we are birds and this is our nest.

## Spider Web

**Collect**

Crepe paper

Several child-sized chairs, placed in a circle, several feet apart

**Do**

Before class, loosely wrap crepe paper around lower portion of chair legs to form a "spider web."

In class, let children climb in and out of the web.

**Say**

Spiders live in webs. Let's pretend to be spiders and crawl around this web.

God made spiders. God made everything that is growing.

Nathanael, you are growing. God made you! Thank You, God, for Nathanael.

## Zoo Animals

**Collect**

Large cardboard blocks

Toy zoo animals

Blue construction paper or fabric to represent water

Green construction paper or fabric to represent grass

**Do**

Help children build animal habitats with the blocks and paper and fabric.

Encourage children to decide which animal goes where.

Children play with animals.

**Say**

Madison, have you ever been to the zoo? What did you see? The giraffe lives near trees.

God made all the animals at the zoo.

God made everything that grows.

## Caring for Animals

**Collect**

April Bible Story Picture from *I Love to Look!* or *Nursery Posters*

Several stuffed toy animals and birds

One or more pet care items (plastic feeding bowls, blankets or pet bed, dog leash, brush)

**Do**

Show and talk about the Bible Story Picture.

Children use materials to pretend to care for pets.

**Say**

Toby, where is the kitty in this picture? God made the animals grow.

What does our kitty need? You can give this kitty a drink of water.

Hope, God made you. You are growing, too! The Bible tells us that God made everything that grows.

**Bonus Idea:** Children pretend to be animals and make animal sounds.

## Animals and Their Babies

**Collect**

April Bible Story Picture from *I Love to Look!* or *Nursery Posters*

**Do**

Show and talk about the Bible Story Picture. Help children match pictures of baby animals to the parents.

**Say**

Andrew, I see a baby cow in this picture. Where is the picture of the cow's mommy? Baby cows grow to be grownup cows. What other baby animals do you see in this picture?

God made all growing things. God made you.

Taylor, you are growing. God made you. Thank You, God, for helping Taylor grow.

**Bonus Idea:** Laminate pictures (from magazines or the Internet) of a variety of animals, one picture of each adult and one of each baby (optional—use clear Con-Tact paper if laminating equipment is not available). Set out pictures and let children match baby animals to the parents.

## Animal Puzzles

**Collect**

Several toddler puzzles depicting animals

**Do**

Children play with the puzzles.

Be ready to help as needed and to talk about the animals.

**Say**

Rachel, you are holding the duck puzzle piece. What does a duck say? Where does the duck puzzle piece go?

God made all the ducks. God made everything that grows!

I see ducks and cows in this puzzle. I see horses and goats. God made all the animals.

## Animal Puppets

**Collect**

Several animal puppets

**Do**

Children use puppets. Be ready to help children put puppets on their hands.

Guide children to make the sound of each animal.

**Say**

Here is a sheep puppet. God made the sheep. God made all growing things.

Darnel, what sound does a sheep make? Is your puppet a baby sheep or a grownup sheep? God makes everything grow.

You are growing. God made you!

## Can You Find It?

**Collect**

Variety of plastic animals and/or insects

Tray

**Do**

Let children help you place all items on the tray.

Ask one child at a time to find a particular animal or insect.

**Say**

Olivia, where is the ladybug? That's it! You found it! God made ladybugs. God made everything that grows.

I see a pig and a horse. Do you see them too? God made baby pigs and baby horses to grow bigger and bigger.

Anthony, God made you. You are growing bigger and bigger, too!

# May

## People at Church Help Me

**Jesus Helped His Friends**
(See John 13:2-5.)

**"God gives people to help me."**
(See 1 Corinthians 12:28.)

**This month you will help each child:**

• hear words and songs about Jesus' help for His friends;

• feel cared for by people at church;

• play with a variety of toys and materials and experience love and help from teachers.

## Devotional

Time in the nursery often seems a bit like a tornado: whoosh, children and parents suddenly arrive; fully absorbed, you whirl and turn and move through a series of caregiving tasks—then suddenly, they are gone! You sit breathlessly, assessing the needed cleanup and asking, "What on earth happened here?"

On such days, it may seem that one task after another took up all your time and energy. Was anything accomplished beyond basic physical care? In some nurseries, no more is expected. But Jesus shows us that in even the most ordinary act of care, there is potential for ministry. When Jesus washed His friends' feet, He taught them not only about being washed physically, but by the way in which He washed their feet, He also taught them the depth of His servanthood and the value He placed on each one of them—even the one who would betray Him. The disciples learned about servanthood and how Jesus valued each of them not by simply having their feet washed, but from the way in which it was done.

You are not merely a provider of services to children. You are a teacher! On the surface, those tasks may seem to involve only the physical care of changing diapers, feeding, playing, cuddling and singing. However, your actions go far beyond mere physical care and become ministry when you use them to express the warmth of Jesus' love. The gentle way in which you talk to, play with and love each child for whom you care teaches each of them something about Jesus' love and about the people at church who love God. That's a powerful lesson!

Such love will radiate from you only as you take time each day to "taste" God's goodness. As you consider His love for you and as you pray for each little one for whom you care, the routine tasks of service to children can become ministry!

During the month of May, display this poster at child's eye level. Talk about the way in which the adult in the poster is demonstrating God's love to the child by playing with him.

## People at Church Help Me

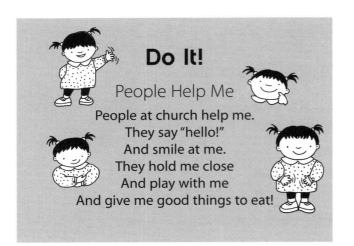

### Do It!

#### People Help Me

People at church help me.
They say "hello!"
And smile at me.
They hold me close
And play with me
And give me good things to eat!

### Sing It!

#### Showing God's Love

(Tune: "Twinkle, Twinkle, Little Star")

I will smile and play with you.
Jesus helped His good friends, too.
I can show I care for you
To help you know that God loves you.

### Tell It!

#### Jesus Helped His Friends

One day Jesus and His friends
Walked and walked.
Their feet were very dirty!
So Jesus helped His friends.
He poured water into a big bowl.
Jesus washed His friends' feet
And dried them with a towel.
Jesus loved to help His friends.
People at church love to help you, too.
(See John 13:2-5.)

Display this poster at teacher's eye level in your nursery. Tell the Bible story, sing the song, do the finger play and repeat the Bible verse to one or more interested children.

## Activities with Children

Choose one or more of the learning activities on pages 75-80 to provide for children during a session. Consider your facility, the number of children and teachers and the supplies you have available as you plan which activities you will use. The best kind of teaching for toddlers will happen as you take advantage of teachable moments as children play and experience the learning activities you have provided. Continue an activity as long as one or more children are interested. For more information on using this curriculum, see "Why Use Curriculum?" on page 8.

## Obstacle Course

**Collect**

Several items for obstacle course (play tunnel, large pillow, hula hoop)

**Do**

Create an obstacle course with the materials. Children walk or crawl through the course. Be ready to help as needed.

**Say**

Michael, you are crawling on our obstacle course. I will help you if you need it.

Jesus helped His friends.

I like to help you.

## Follow the Footprints

**Collect**

May Bible Story Picture from *I Love to Look!* or *Nursery Posters*

Pencil

Shoes

Construction paper or card stock

Scissors

Laminating equipment or clear Con-Tact paper

Masking tape

**Do**

Before class, trace around a pair of shoes on paper or card stock to make 10 left feet and 10 right feet. Cut out and laminate or cover with clear Con-Tact paper. Tape feet to the floor of your classroom in a way that creates a walking path.

In class, show and talk about the Bible Story Picture.

Walk on the path together with children.

**Say**

Let's follow this path together. I will help you, Joseph and Mark. Sophie, I will help you, too.

I'm glad to help our friends at church.

Jesus helped His friends, too. Look at this picture. One day Jesus and His friends walked and walked. Their feet were very dirty! Jesus washed His friends' feet.

## Toddler Limbo

**Collect**

Measuring stick or broom handle to use as a limbo stick

**Do**

With another teacher, hold each end of the limbo stick at about the children's height.

Children walk under the stick.

After the children walk under it once, lower the stick slightly and ask them to do it again. Continue lowering the stick until children must crawl, or until they lose interest.

**Say**

Mrs. Lucas and I are going to help you play a game. We're happy to help you.

At church we like to play with you and help you.

Thank You, God, for our friends at church.

## Block Towers

**Collect**

Blocks

**Do**

Build a tower with a child, taking turns to add blocks. Encourage several interested children to build a tower together.

**Say**

Let's see if we can help each other build a tower. Sara, you can put the first block on the floor. James, you can put the next block. And I'll put the third block on our tower. One, two, three!

Thank you for helping, Sara and James.

People at church help each other. Jesus helped His friends, too.

## Washing Toys

**Collect**

May Bible Story Picture from *I Love to Look!* or *Nursery Posters*

One or two dishpans with small amount of soapy water

Washable classroom toys

Several washcloths or paper towels

Towels

**Do**

Show and talk about the Bible Story Picture.

Let children help you wash and dry the toys. (Optional: Children pretend to wash and dry toys.)

**Say**

Bryce, look at this picture of Jesus and His friends. Jesus washed His friends' feet when they were dirty. Jesus loved to help His friends.

We have toys at church for you to play with. Sometimes they get dirty. Let's help each other wash them.

At church we help our friends. We help each other. Thank You, God, for people who help us.

## "People at Church Help Me" Picture

**Collect**

9x12-inch (23x30.5-cm) sheet of construction paper for each child

Pictures of jackets, shoes, snacks and storybooks, cut from catalogs

Glue sticks

Marker

**Do**

Before class, print the words "People at Church Help Me" at the top of each papers.

In class help children glue pictures to their papers.

Talk about the items in the pictures and how people use them at church.

**Say**

Jacqueline, you glued a picture of goldfish crackers to your paper. I'm glad to help you have crackers to eat at church.

Laura, can you point to the picture of the jacket? You have a jacket just like that! When we go outside, I will help you put your jacket on. I like you and I'm glad you came today.

I like to help you. Friends at church like to help each other.

## Foot Tracing

**Collect**

9x12-inch (23x30.5-cm) sheet of construction paper for each child

Crayons

**Do**

Trace around children's feet on the papers. (Optional: Help children remove shoes and socks.)

**Say**

Let's make a drawing of your feet. I will help you.

Look! There are your two feet.

Gerardo, I 'm glad you came today. I'm glad to help you.

## Mother's Day Card

**Collect**

8½x11-inch (21.5x28-cm) sheet of white card stock for each child

Heart and flower stickers

**Do**

Before class, fold sheet of card stock in half to make a card. Print "Happy Mother's Day" on front of card. Print "I'm glad God made you my mommy" on inside of card. Make a card for each child. (Optional: Unfold card and photocopy to make one card for each child.)

In class, children decorate cards with stickers.

Read the words to the child and write child's name inside card.

**Say**

This is a special card you can make to give to your mom.

I will be glad to help you make your card.

I like to be with you at church, Samantha. Jesus loves you!

## Cornstarch Goop

**Collect**

Box of cornstarch
Shallow pan or tray
Water
Towels

**Do**

Before class, pour cornstarch onto pan or tray. Add water slowly and stir until mixture thickens.

In class, begin playing with mixture and invite interested children to touch and play with the mixture.

**Say**

Today we're making "goop." Let's mix it together with our hands.

When we're done playing with the goop, I will help you wash your hands.

One time Jesus washed His friends' feet. Jesus liked to help His friends. I like helping you.

## Wet Rocks

**Collect**

Variety of rocks placed on a large tray
Two spray bottles filled with water

**Do**

Children spray the rocks with water.
Help children describe the changes they see.

**Say**

Charis, let's spray the rocks. I will be happy to help you.

What is happening to the rocks? The water makes them look shiny.

You're having fun at church with your friends. I'm glad to help you all.

## Personal Pizzas

**Note:** Post a note alerting parents to the use of food. Also, check children's registration forms for possible food allergies.

**Collect**

May Bible Story Picture from *I Love to Look!* or *Nursery Posters*

Round crackers
Cheese spread
Plastic knives

**Do**

Show and talk about the Bible Story Picture. Help one child at a time use a plastic knife to spread small amount of cheese spread on a cracker.

Children eat crackers.

**Say**

Today I can help you make a cheese snack.

I'm glad to help you. I like you! Thank You, God, for all our friends at church today.

Jesus helped His friends, too. Look at this picture of Jesus. He helped His friends by washing their feet. Then He dried them with a towel. Jesus loved His friends.

## Water Movement

**Collect**

Several water bottles filled with color water and an interesting item to look at (two or three marbles, beads or buttons, spoonful of glitter, etc.) and then securely fastened with glue and tape

**Do**

Let children experiment with and play with water bottles. Talk about what the children see.

When a child hands a bottle to you or another child, comment on the way he or she is helping.

**Say**

Lauren, you're having fun shaking the bottle. When you are done, please hand the bottle to Marcos.

At church, we can help each other. Thank you, Lauren, for giving your bottle to Marcos.

I'm glad to be at church! I'm glad we can help each other at church.

**Bonus Idea:** Put a variety of small plastic fish into the water bottles.

## Marching Band

**Collect**

*I Love to Sing!* CD (or other recorded music with a marching beat) and player
Rhythm instruments

**Do**

Let each child choose an instrument.
Play "Helping" or other music.
March with children around the room.

**Say**

Let's be in a marching band together.
Which instrument do you want? This is how you play it.
I like helping you at church. I'm glad you are here today.
**Bonus Idea:** Lead children in moving in different ways around the room: baby steps, giant steps, tiptoe, etc.

## People at Church Help Me

**Collect**

May Bible Story Picture from *I Love to Look!* or *Nursery Posters*

**Do**

Show and talk about the Bible Story Picture.
Sing the following words to the tune of "London Bridge":

> People at church help me today,
> when I eat, when I play.
> People help me every day.
> Thank You, God.

**Say**

Look at this picture of Jesus and His friends. Jesus helped His friends when they were together. People at church help you when we're together.
Let's sing a song about the people who help us at church. Mrs. Smith helps us have a good snack to eat. I'm glad that people at church help us.

Reverend Dan teaches us about God. There are so many people at church who help us. Thank You, God, for people who help us.
**Bonus Idea:** Collect pictures of people children regularly see at church (teachers, pastor, parents of their friends, etc.). Show pictures to children as you sing about people who help them at church.

## Sing with Streamers

**Collect**

*I Love to Sing!* CD (or other recorded music) and player
Two 18-inch (45.5-cm) lengths of crepe paper for each child

**Do**

As you play "Together" or other music, children wave the crepe paper, twirl it, etc.

**Say**

Here are some streamers, Allie. I made them for you. I'm glad to help you.
When we are at church, we can help our friends.
I'm glad you are here at church today. I will help you when you need it.

## Jingle Bell Walk

**Collect**

One or two jingle bells (too large to swallow) for each child
Chenille wire in a variety of colors

**Do**

If a child is interested, thread bell onto chenille wire and wrap around a child's wrist or ankle.

**Say**

Let's wear these jingle bells. I'll help you put the bell around your ankle. When you walk, you'll play the bells!
I see our friends Victoria, Ian and Alex. I'm glad to help you all!

## Cross the River

**Collect**

Blue fabric sheet
Several carpet squares

**Do**

Place sheet on floor. Arrange carpet squares on the sheet, forming a path from one side of the sheet to the other. Help children pretend to cross the river by stepping on the "rocks."

**Say**

Torrie, let's pretend this sheet is a river. We can cross the river by stepping on the rocks. Would you like me to help you cross the river?

People at church help you. I'm glad you are here. I'm glad to help you.

## A Long Road

**Collect**

May Bible Story Picture from *I Love to Look!* or *Nursery Posters*
Large cardboard blocks
Toy people

**Do**

Show and talk about the Bible Story Picture.

Help children lay blocks end to end to build a long road. Children pretend to "walk" the people on the road.

**Say**

The Bible tells us that Jesus loved His friends. One day Jesus and His friends walked and walked on a road. Their feet got very dirty. Jesus helped His friends. He washed their feet.

Let's build a long road today. I will help you. Then we can pretend these people are walking on the road.

Sean, I'm glad you are here today. I love you. Thank You, God, for Sean.

## Who's the Cook?

**Collect**

Plastic bowls and spoons
Dolls

**Do**

Children pretend to cook food and serve it to their dolls.

**Say**

Caitlin, you are stirring the bowl. What are you cooking? Your mom and dad cook your food at home.

I'm glad moms and dads help us. People at church help us, too.

## Mail Carrier

**Collect**

Large purse to represent mail bag
Junk mail
Several large mailing envelopes

**Do**

Put mail in bag and "deliver" some to each child.

Let children take a turn to deliver the mail if they wish.

**Say**

Who brings the mail to your house? Mail carriers help us.

People at church help us, too. I'll help you by giving you some mail to deliver.

It's fun to be at church. I like to be with you at church.

**Bonus Idea:** Provide discarded envelopes and stickers. Children put stickers on envelopes.

## Lacing

**Collect**
Paper plates
Hole punch
Long shoe laces (or yarn with ends taped)

**Do**
Before class, punch holes around edge of paper plates. Attach a shoe lace to each plate.
In class, help children insert laces in and out of the holes (using any sequence of holes).

**Say**
Would you like to put the laces around this plate? I will be glad to help you do it.
People at church are glad to help you.

## Happy to Help

**Collect**
May Bible Story Picture from *I Love to Look!* or *Nursery Posters*
Four large paper plates
Markers in four colors

**Do**
Before class, draw a happy face on each plate, using a different color for each face.
In class, show and talk about the Bible Story Picture.
Place plates facedown. Children turn over plates. Identify the color of each happy face.

**Say**
Gerardo, where is Jesus in this picture? There He is! He is helped His friends. His friends had dirty feet. Jesus washed their feet.
When someone helps us, it makes us happy. Let's see how many happy faces we can find. Tell me the color of the happy face you find.
Thank You, God, for people at church who love us and help us.
**Bonus Idea:** Hide plates in the room for children to find.

## Who Helps Me?

**Collect**
Items used in your class collected in a basket or bag (child's shoe, child's sweater, name tag, paper cup, storybook, etc.)

**Do**
Let one child at a time remove an item from the basket or bag.

**Say**
Devin, you are holding the shoe. Mrs. Barber helps you put on your shoes when you are at church.
Jillian, who helped you put on your name tag today? That's right! It was Mrs. Davis.
People at church help you.

## Community Workers

**Collect**
One or more sturdy books with pictures of community workers such as doctor, mail carrier, trash truck driver, restaurant server, grocery worker

**Do**
Look at books with children. Talk about the pictures. Read the text if children are interested.

**Say**
Jacob, let's read this book about the firefighter. Firefighters help us! People at church help you, too!
Kaylie, I like looking at this book with you. I see a picture of a doctor helping a little boy.
It's fun to look at books together at church. I like helping you.

# June

## God Cares for Me

### Jesus Told About God's Care
(See Matthew 6:28-32.)

### "God cares about you."
(See 1 Peter 5:7.)

### This month you will help each child:
• hear words and songs about God's care for him or her;

• feel thankful for God's care;

• participate in play activities to learn ways God cares for him or her.

## Devotional

It's easy to see how God could care for the young children in our care: sweet and happy, they delight us with their excitement over everyday things. It's a joy to tell them of His love as we play with them and care for them. No doubt God cares for them even more than we do! But what kind of care does God have for us grown-ups? Let's look at Peter's statement in 1 Peter 5:7: "Cast all your anxiety on him because he cares for you."

How much worrying do you think young children do? Do you suppose they wake in the morning, stressed over where their food will come from? Does their blood pressure rise as they fret over the possible problems of the day? Here they are, dependent on the caregivers—and instead of being stressed about their dependency, they respond in a blessed confidence, nestling in the arms of one who loves them and falling asleep in a relaxed lump of total trust. That's not just a sweet picture; it's the reality of God's care!

Now take a moment to think about the anxieties you faced this week: from the plumbing to the trouble your child had at school to worries about whether or not the groceries will stretch until payday. Adult lives seem to swell with anxiety-producing situations! Our blood pressure rises, our stomachs churn—and all the while, God invites us with open arms to give our anxieties to Him, relax in that child-like blessed confidence and stop losing sleep over our troubles! Perhaps we don't play with excitement as well as we once did, but God wants us to remember that no matter how big and responsible we are, we're still His little ones. He is willing—and waiting—to care for our anxiety. So give your anxieties to Him. Rest in Him. He cares for you!

During the month of June, display this poster at child's eye level. Talk about God's care for flowers and His wonderful love and care for children.

## Do It!

### God Cares for Me

God cares for me
When I sleep.
God cares for me
When I play.
God cares for me
All the time,
Every night and
Every day.

## Sing It!

### I'm So Glad

(Tune: "Skip to My Lou")

I'm so glad that God loves me, God
loves me, God loves me.
I'm so glad that God loves me, He loves
me all the time.
I'm so glad that God loves you, God
loves you, God loves you.
I'm so glad that God loves you, He loves
you all the time.

## Tell It!

### Jesus Told About God's Care

"Look at the pretty flowers,"
Jesus said.
"God makes them grow.
He makes red, yellow and white flowers.
God made these flowers,
And He cares for them.
God made you.
God loves you and cares for you, too.
God loves you even more than flowers."
(See Matthew 6:28-32.)

Display this poster at teacher's eye level in your nursery. Tell the Bible story, sing the song, do the finger play and repeat the Bible verse to one or more interested children.

## Activities with Children

Choose one or more of the learning activities on pages 83-88 to provide for children during a session. Consider your facility, the number of children and teachers and the supplies you have available as you plan which activities you will use. The best kind of teaching for toddlers will happen as you take advantage of teachable moments as children play and experience the learning activities you have provided. Continue an activity as long as one or more children are interested. For more information on using this curriculum, see "Why Use Curriculum?" on page 8.

## Seed to Flower

**Collect**

Packet of flower seeds
Empty watering can

**Do**

Show children a packet of flower seeds. Take out a seed to show how small it is. Tell them the seed needs water and sunshine to grow into a flower.

Children crouch down to make themselves small, like seeds.

Pretend to water the "seeds" with watering can. Children stretch up and pretend to be flowers.

**Say**

Look at these small flower seeds. When we plant the seeds and water them, they will grow into flowers like the picture on the seed packet.

You can pretend to be a seed. I'll pretend to water you so you will grow into a flower.

Jesus said that God cares for the flowers. God gives them rain and sunshine so they will grow.

Jesus said that God cares for you, too.

**Bonus Idea:** Plant seeds in an outdoor area near your classroom, or in pots that can be kept indoors.

## God Gives Me Food

**Collect**

Toy food and/or empty food containers
One or more large baskets

**Do**

Place food items in various places around the room.

Ask children to find foods and name them.

Ask children to place the foods in the baskets.

**Say**

God gives us lots of good food. God cares for us.

Let's find some pretend food and put it in this basket.

What did you find, Mariah? God gives us apples because He cares for us.

## Watering Flowers

**Collect**

June Bible Story Picture from *I Love to Look!* or *Nursery Posters*

One or more small watering cans filled part way with water

Several flowering plants

**Do**

Show and talk about the Bible Story Picture.

Children water plants. (Optional: Take children outside to water plants in an enclosed play area.)

**Say**

Jesus told people that God cares for flowers and God cares for us. Thank You, God, for caring for us.

Let's water the flowers. Flowers need water to grow.

God sends rain to water the flowers He made.

## Bees and Flowers

**Collect**

Poster board in assorted colors
Scissors

**Do**

Before class, cut large flower shapes from poster board.

In class, place flowers on the floor.

Encourage children to "fly" from flower to flower like bees.

**Say**

Let's fly like bees. Bees like flowers. We can fly to the pink flower and then to the red flower.

God made the flowers and He cares for them.

God made you and He cares for you.

## "God Cares for Me" Picture

**Collect**

12x18-inch (30.5x45.5-cm) sheet of construction paper for each child
Marker
Pictures of people and food, cut from magazines
Glue sticks

**Do**

Before class, cut each sheet of construction paper into the shape of a house. Print the words "God cares for me" on each house.

In class, help one child at a time glue pictures onto a house.

**Say**

These words say, "God cares for me."

Hunter, God cares for you. You are gluing a picture of a dad on your house. God gives you a family because He cares about you. Thank You, God, for dads.

Trevor, you have the picture of spaghetti. God gives you food. God cares for you.

## Flower Garden

**Collect**

Large plastic or paper cups
Artificial flowers with stems

**Do**

Let children put flowers into and out of cups, pretending to plant, pick and then replant flowers.

**Say**

Look at all the flowers in our garden. God made flowers.

God made dirt for the flowers to grow in. God is good. He cares for us.

## Finger Fun

**Collect**

June Bible Story Picture from *I Love to Look!* or *Nursery Posters*
Paper
Jumbo crayons

**Do**

Children color on paper. Talk about the flowers God made in the colors used by children.

Show and talk about the Bible Story Picture.

**Say**

Anthony, you are drawing with the red crayon. God made red flowers.

Look at the picture of Jesus. Jesus told people that God cares for us all the time. God cares for flowers. God cares for us even more!

Thank You, God, for loving us.

## Father's Day Card

**Collect**

8½x11-inch (21.5x28-cm) sheet of card stock or construction paper for each child, folded in half
Marker
Stickers
Crayons

**Do**

Write "I love you, Daddy" or other greeting inside the card. Encourage child to add decorations with stickers or crayons.

Write child's name. Trace child's hand with crayon.

**Say**

Would you like to make your daddy (uncle, grandpa, etc.) a card?

We can put your handprint on the front.

Your daddy cares for you. So does God!

**Bonus Idea:** Glue a photo of each child to the inside of the card.

## Flowering Plants

**Collect**

One or more flowering plants in pots

**Do**

Place plants on a child-sized table where children can see them.

Help children notice differences in the plants. Place plants out of reach when adult supervision is not available.

**Say**

God made so many kinds of flowers.

He gives them water and sun and dirt to grow in.

God cares for flowers. God cares for you, too.

## Flower Petals

**Collect**

June Bible Story Picture from *I Love to Look!* or *Nursery Posters*

Flower petals in a plastic jar

**Do**

Show and talk about the Bible Story Picture.

Let children take petals out of the jar, feel them, smell them and return petals to jar.

**Say**

Gabriel, look at the pretty pink flowers God made. Do you see a pink flower in this picture?

Jesus said that God cares for flowers. God cares for us even more!

Thank You, God, for Your care.

**Bonus Idea:** Take pictures of the flowers with a digital or instant camera to display in the classroom.

## Edible Flowers

**Note:** Post a note alerting parents to the use of food. Also, check children's registration forms for possible food allergies.

**Collect**

Broccoli and cauliflower, cut into small pieces

**Do**

Show children the broccoli and cauliflower.

Give interested children small pieces to touch and taste.

**Say**

This is broccoli. It's a flower we can eat.

Calvin, would you like a taste?

God gives you good food. God cares for you.

## What's in the Bag?

**Collect**

Variety of 4-inch (10-cm) fabric squares in different colors and textures

Bag

**Do**

One at a time, place a fabric square into the bag.

Children take turns looking into the bag and then taking out the fabric square.

**Say**

Xavier, you used your eyes to look into the bag. Then you used your hand to take the red cloth out of the bag. God made your hands. God cares for you!

God gives us what we need! God loves us very much!

## Walking, Walking

**Collect**

June Bible Story Picture from *I Love to Look!* or *Nursery Posters*
*I Love to Sing!* CD and player
Several dolls

**Do**

Show and talk about the Bible Story Picture.
Play "I See You!" on CD. Children walk around the room holding dolls.

**Say**

Jesus told people that God cares about them. How many children do you see in this picture? God cares about you, too!

Mia, you are having fun walking with your doll. God made your legs so you can walk. God cares for you.

Blake, you are taking good care of your doll. God cares for you.

**Bonus Idea:** Lead children on a walk outdoors in an enclosed play area.

## God Cares for Me

**Do**

Sing the following words to the tune of "God Is So Good" during teachable moments while you are playing with a child, or while eating a snack with a child:

God cares for me. God cares for me.
God cares for me. He's so good to me.

Additional verses: God gives me food. God gives me love. God gives me friends.

**Say**

I'm so glad that God cares for us! Let's sing about the good things God gives us.

Ellie, God gives you lots of friends here at church. God cares for you.

## Fingers, Nose and Toes

**Do**

Sing the following words to the tune of "If You're Happy and You Know It":

Put your fingers on your nose
and then your toes.
Put your fingers on your nose
and then your toes.
Put your fingers on your nose,
put your fingers on your nose.
Put your fingers on your nose
and then your toes.

**Say**

God made us. God cares about us!
God made our noses. God made our toes.
Thank You, God, for caring about us.

## Drum Music

**Collect**

*I Love to Sing!* CD and player
Round, empty oatmeal boxes (or other cylinders)
Construction paper
Scissors
Tape or glue
Stickers

**Do**

Before class, tape or glue lids to oatmeal boxes. Cut paper to fit around the boxes. Glue or tape paper securely to boxes.

In class, children attach stickers to their drums.

Play "All I Need" and let children pat drums with their hands.

**Say**

Let's make some drums. We'll use our drums when we sing about God's care for us.

I'm glad you came today, Carlos. I care about you! God cares about you, too!

## Hats for You and Me

**Collect**

Washable sun hats or plastic visors
One or two beach towels

**Do**

Interested children put on hats and sit on beach towels, pretending they are going swimming.

**Say**

Toby, let's pretend we're going swimming. Let's sit on our beach towel. Which hat do you want to wear?

God cares for you. God loves you very much. God loves us wherever we go.

## Play House

**Collect**

Large cardboard appliance carton
Utility knife
Carpet square
Markers or non-toxic paints and paintbrushes

**Do**

Before class, cut windows and a door in the carton. Place carpet square on inside of carton on "floor." Decorate outside of carton with markers or paint.

In class, children play inside the "house."

**Say**

Let's pretend this is our house. Who would like to go inside?

God gave you a home to live in.

God cares for you. I'm glad God cares for you. I'm glad God cares for me!

## Gardening

**Collect**

June Bible Story Picture from *I Love to Look!* or *Nursery Posters*
Toy garden tools
Watering can
Silk flowers and/or plants

**Do**

Show and talk about the Bible Story Picture. Children pretend to be gardeners by using the tools and watering the flowers.

**Say**

Chloe, where are the red flowers in this picture? That's right! Jesus said that God cares for the flowers. God cares for us, too.

Let's pretend we are gardeners. Micah, where should we grow our plants? We can take care of our plants by watering them.

God takes care of us, too. God loves us! Thank You, God, for Your love.

## God Gave Me a Family

**Collect**

Toy house and people

**Do**

Children play with toy house and people.

**Say**

Ariel, who are you putting in the house?

God gave you a family to love you. God cares for you.

## Flower Sort

### Collect
Plastic or silk flowers (no small parts) in a variety of colors, at least two of each color

### Do
Children play with and sort the flowers. Talk about flowers whose colors match. (Note: Many young children are just beginning to distinguish colors.)

### Say
Sophie, this flower is red. Can you find another red flower? Here it is. Let's put them together.

God made so many pretty flowers. God cares for the flowers. God cares for you.

**Bonus Idea:** Help interested children match flowers to colors of toys in the room.

## Shape Fun

### Collect
June Bible Story Picture from *I Love to Look!* or *Nursery Posters*

Shapes (triangle, circle, star) approximately 3 inches (7.5 cm) in size made from a variety of colored card stock

### Do
Show and talk about the Bible Story Picture.

Children play with the shapes. Talk with children about the colors of the shapes, count the shapes, etc.

### Say
Alyssa, where is the tree in this picture? Where is Jesus? "Look at the pretty flowers," Jesus said. "God cares for them." Then Jesus told people that God loves them, even more than flowers!

God cares about you. God made your eyes so you can see so many things.

William, can you point to the triangle? That's right! There it is. God made your eyes. God cares about you! Thank You, God, for Your love and care.

## "God Cares for Me" Game

### Collect
Pictures (from magazines or Internet) of food, clothes, families and homes
Laminating equipment or clear Con-Tact paper
Box with a lid, large enough to hold the pictures
Heart cut from red construction paper
Marker
Glue

### Do
Before class, laminate or cover pictures with Con-Tact paper to protect them. Print "God cares for me" on the heart. Glue the heart to the top of the lid. Place pictures inside the box.

Let one child at a time choose a picture from the box.

### Say
Let's see how God cares for you, Kyle. You can take a picture out of the box. I see you found the picture of apples. God gives you good food to eat. God cares for you by giving you what you need to grow.

Katie, you found the picture of the family. God gives you a family. God cares about you.

## Sharing Books

### Collect
Sturdy picture books with simple text about God's love and care

### Do
Look at the pictures in a book with one or two children at a time. Read the text to interested children.

### Say
Michael, the boys and girls in this picture are friends. God gives us friends to play with.

I'm so glad God cares for you and me.

Thank You, God, for giving us so many good things.

# July

## God Made Me

### God Made Everything
(See Psalm 95:3-7.)

### "God made me."
(See Job 33:4.)

• • • • • • • • • • • •

**This month you will help each child:**

• hear words and songs about God making people;

• feel glad for his or her amazing body;

• participate in a variety of fun activities and enjoy using his or her body.

## Devotional

Perhaps Adam felt like a child with a new toy when the Lord brought the animals for him to name. What an array of creatures! All shapes, sizes, colors—each one was uniquely fascinating, deserving of extended scrutiny. Imagine Adam's delight as he first stroked the lion's mane, admired a peacock as its tail fanned out, observed a monkey's antics. Yet even as Adam delighted in each new form of life, God was aware that none of these creatures could ever be a suitable companion for Adam. Only another human could meet Adam's wide range of needs and interests.

Every descendant of Adam and Eve carries the same need for human companionship. While the child's intense curiosity can be satisfied with toys, pictures, books and animals, contact with people remains his or her overpowering interest. Just as God recognized Adam's need, adults who care for young children must recognize that each child needs the companionship of a caring person. Meeting that need calls for giving more than bottles or crackers. It requires patient and understanding adults who give themselves willingly to the task of showing God's love to each of His little ones.

During the month of July, display this poster at child's eye level. Describe what the child in the poster is doing and how God's love is shown in the way He made us.

## Do It!

### God Made

God made my ears.
God made my nose.
God made my fingers.
God made my toes.
God made my eyes.
They're both open wide.
God made my mouth
With a tongue inside!

## Sing It!

### I Have Two Eyes

(Tune: "Pop Goes the Weasel")

I have two eyes.
I have two ears.
I have two hands and feet.
I have one mouth
And one little nose,
But, oh, so many fingers and toes!

## Tell It!

### God Made People

God made everything!
God made the cold water we drink.
God made the big waves in the sea.
God made the land that's all around us.
God made all the people, too—
Big ones and little ones,
People like me, and people like you.
God made us. And we are glad!
(See Psalm 95:3-7.)

Display this poster at teacher's eye level in your nursery. Tell the Bible story, sing the song, do the finger play and repeat the Bible verse to one or more interested children.

## Activities with Children

Choose one or more of the learning activities on pages 91-96 to provide for children during a session. Consider your facility, the number of children and teachers and the supplies you have available as you plan which activities you will use. The best kind of teaching for toddlers will happen as you take advantage of teachable moments as children play and experience the learning activities you have provided. Continue an activity as long as one or more children are interested. For more information on using this curriculum, see "Why Use Curriculum?" on page 8.

## Touch Your Toes

**Do**

Lead one to three children to play Simon Says, without ever omitting the phrase "Simon Says" so that no children are eliminated.

Use actions such as "touch your toes," "stamp your feet," "wave your arms," "bend your knees," "pat your head." Repeat as long as children are interested.

**Say**

Let's play a fun game. Can you do what I am doing? Simon Says touch your toes. God made your toes.

Tyler, you waved your arms. God made your arms. God made every part of you.

We're stamping our feet. Thank You, God, for making our feet.

## Follow the Line

**Collect**

Masking tape

**Do**

Before class, make a masking tape line that turns several times on the floor of your room. (Remove tape after session.)

In class, ask children to follow the line in a variety of ways: walking, crawling, jumping, etc.

**Say**

God made you. God made your legs. You can follow this line by jumping.

Damon, you like to jump! God gave you legs for kicking. God gave you feet for walking.

God made your eyes so you can see the line. God made you!

## Basketball

**Collect**

July Bible Story Picture from *I Love to Look!* or *Nursery Posters*
Large basket
Several soft balls

**Do**

Show and talk about the Bible Story Picture.
Place basket on floor (or outdoors) in an open area.

Give children balls and let them toss balls into the basket.

**Say**

Look at the children in this picture. The Bible tells us that God made us. God made your hands. God made your arms.

Nicole, you threw the ball right into the basket! God made your arms.

## Climbing

**Collect**

Climbing structure

**Do**

Take children outdoors to an enclosed play area.
Encourage interested children to climb on climbing structure.

**Say**

God made you. He gave you strong legs for climbing.

Michael, you are using your arms to climb. You are using your legs to climb. God made every part of you.

God made your legs so you can climb.

**Bonus Idea:** Attach a colorful ribbon to fence or climbing structure. Invite interested children to run to the ribbon and back again.

## I Can See

### Collect

July Bible Story Picture from *I Love to Look!* or *Nursery Posters*

Variety of non-breakable interesting things to look at such as colorful shakers, kaleidoscopes, hour glasses, prisms, snow globes

### Do

Show and talk about the Bible Story Picture.

Encourage children to look at and experiment with the items you collected.

Talk about what they see.

### Say

I see some water in this picture. I see a tree, too! God made my eyes. God made your eyes, too!

Braden, you are looking at the pretty colors. I see red. I see yellow. God made your eyes to see colors.

## I Can Touch

### Collect

White glue

Margarine tubs

9x12-inch (23x30.5-cm) sheet of construction paper for each child

Marker

Scraps of materials with different textures (sandpaper, fabric, foil, fur, etc.).

1-inch (2.5-cm) foam brushes

### Do

Before class, pour some glue in each margarine tub. Print "I Can Touch" on top of each paper.

In class, help one child at a time to use brushes to spread glue on paper and place scraps on the glue.

Help child feel and describe each scrap before it is placed on paper.

### Say

Kelly, you are holding the sandpaper. It feels rough.

I like to feel this soft fabric. God made our hands to feel things.

God made you!

**Bonus Idea:** Help each child glue a material onto a sheet of card stock. Staple several sheets together to make a book.

## I Can Taste

**Note:** Post a note alerting parents to the use of food. Also, check children's registration forms for possible food allergies.

### Collect

Variety of finger foods such as O-shaped cereal, raisins, small pieces of cheese, etc.

Napkins and small plates

### Do

Give children a variety of foods to taste.

Talk about the foods' characteristics (sweet, salty, crunchy, etc.).

### Say

These raisins are sweet. Ava, do you want to taste some cheese?

God made your mouth to taste and eat good food. Thank You, God, for making our mouths.

I'm glad God made you.

## I Can Smell

### Collect

Variety of spices in plastic jars with lids

### Do

Remove the lid of one spice at a time and invite a few children to smell it.

Place spices out of reach when not being used with children.

### Say

Madeline, this is cinnamon. It smells good! Would you like to smell it?

God gave you a nose to smell things.

God made you. God made your arms (touch child's arm), your head (touch child's head) and your hands (touch child's hand).

## Color Mixing

**Collect**

Three one-gallon resealable freezer bags
Red, blue and yellow tempera paint
Tablespoon
Masking tape

**Do**

Before class, place one tablespoon red and one tablespoon yellow paint in first bag, squeeze out air and close tightly. Repeat with one tablespoon red and one tablespoon blue paint in a second bag, and then one tablespoon blue and one tablespoon yellow paint in a third bag. Tape bags to a child-sized table.

In class, as children look at the bags, name the colors of the paints.

Children mix the colors with their fingers. Name the new (secondary) colors that form.

**Say**

Aiden, let's use our fingers to mix the red and yellow paint together. Look! Now we have orange!

God gave you eyes to see colors. God made your fingers and hands, too.

God made you.

## Feel Your Breath

**Collect**

Cotton balls

**Do**

Show children how to blow on their hands to feel their breath.

Let children blow cotton balls across a child-sized table.

**Say**

Alyssa, can you blow on your hands like this? God made your hands so that they can feel lots of things.

I'm glad God made our hands. God made us!

**Bonus Idea:** Provide several large feathers for children to blow.

## Beautiful Me

**Collect**

July Bible Story Picture from *I Love to Look!* or *Nursery Posters*
Unbreakable mirror

**Do**

Show and talk about the Bible Story Picture.

Have one child at a time look in the mirror.

Point out child's distinguishing characteristics.

**Say**

The Bible tells us that God made us. There are two children in this picture. Their hair is brown! God made you, Lily. Your hair is red.

Who it that in the mirror? Yes, it's you, Gianna! God made you. God gave you blue eyes. God gave you brown hair.

Now, who is in the mirror? Look, it's Connor! God made you, Connor.

## Fingerprints

**Collect**

Stamp pad with washable ink
White paper
Magnifying glass
Premoistened towelettes

**Do**

Children place fingers on stamp pad and then on paper. Wash hands with towelettes.

Let children look at their fingerprints through a magnifying glass.

**Say**

God made your fingers. Let's make our fingerprints.

Hailey, you can use the magnifying glass to see your fingerprints.

God made your fingers. God made your toes. God made all of you. Thank You, God, for making us.

## What Do You Hear?

**Collect**

Five or six rhythm instruments (drum, bells, shakers, tambourine, sticks, triangle)

**Do**

Let children play the instruments. Tell children the names of the instruments. Some children may be able to repeat the names.

Hold an instrument behind your back, play it and ask children to guess which instrument it is. If children do not guess, bring instrument out, tell the name, and play it.

Continue with other instruments.

**Say**

Abigail, which instrument do you hear? That's right—it's the bells!

You heard the bells with your ears. God made your ears. God made you.

God gave you ears to hear things.

## Freeze Dance

**Collect**

*I Love to Sing!* CD and player

**Do**

Play "God Made Me" and walk around the room, clapping and moving in time to the music.

Pause the music, stop moving and say "freeze." Model what this means by staying in place until music starts again.

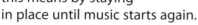

Continue as long as children are interested.

**Say**

Let's play a freeze game. When you hear the music, you can move around the room.

God gave us bodies that can move. God made us.

God made our legs that move. God made our hands that can clap. Thank You, God!

## God Made My Eyes

**Do**

Sing the following song to the tune of "God Is So Good":

God made my eyes. God made my eyes.
God made my eyes, so I can see.

Repeat song, using words such as:

God made my ears, so I can hear
God made my nose, so I can smell
God made my hands, so I can touch
God made my feet, so I can walk

**Say**

Let's sing about the things God made. God made every part of you!

## Body Parts

**Collect**

July Bible Story Picture from *I Love to Look!* or *Nursery Posters*

*I Love to Sing!* CD (or other recorded music that directs children to clap hands, stomp feet, etc.) and player

**Do**

Show and talk about the Bible Story Picture. Play "Watch Me" or other music.

Follow the directions to move various body parts, and encourage children to follow along, too.

**Say**

The little girl in this picture is having fun. She is putting her feet in the water. The Bible tells us that God made her feet.

We can have fun clapping our hands and stomping our feet. God made our hands. God made our feet.

God made each one of us. Thank You, God, for making Isabella. Thank You, God, for making Logan.

## What Did You Wear?

**Collect**

Large unbreakable mirror (full-length if possible)

**Do**

Children look in the mirror. Talk about what the child is wearing.

**Say**

Jacob, you're wearing a blue shirt today. God gives you clothes to keep your body warm. God made you.

Brianna, look in the mirror. What are you wearing today? I see your pink dress. I see your arms and legs. God made you!

**Bonus Idea:** Help interested children look to see who else is wearing the same color of clothing.

## My House

**Collect**

Wooden blocks
Photo of each child in the class
Clear packaging tape

**Do**

Before class, tape each child's photo to a block.

In class, children build houses with blocks. Ask each child to find his or her picture to put in a house.

**Say**

God made children. God made you. Let's find your picture.

Mia, you found your picture. Benjamin, you found your picture, too!

Thank You, God, for Mia and Benjamin.

## What Can I Be?

**Collect**

One or more hats that represent occupations

**Do**

Children try on hats.

**Say**

Riley, you are wearing the firefighter hat. Grace, you are wearing the captain's hat.

It's fun to wear hats. We wear hats on our heads. God made our heads. God made our whole bodies.

## Exercise Fun

**Collect**

July Bible Story Picture from *I Love to Look!* or *Nursery Posters*

**Do**

Show and talk about the Bible Story Picture.

Guide children to do large body movements (reach high, touch toes, run in place, sit-ups, etc.).

**Say**

Let's count how many people are in this picture. God made dads. God made children.

Let's pretend that we are at the park today. (Optional: Go outdoors in an enclosed play area.) What will we do at the park? God made our arms that reach up high. God made our feet that can run.

Our bodies need to move and exercise. Some moms and dads go to exercise classes. We can exercise, too!

## Put Me Together

**Collect**

Felt squares in several skin colors
Scissors
Flannel board

**Do**

Before class, cut a large figure of a person from each felt square. Cut all but one person into these sections: head, torso and arms, legs.

Help one child at a time put the person together on the flannel board.

**Say**

God made people. Let's put together this puzzle of a person.

Zachary, you have the arms for the person. Where do the arms go? God made your arms.

Look, we put together the person! God made people. God made you!

## Can You Feel It?

**Collect**

July Bible Story Picture from *I Love to Look!* or *Nursery Posters*
Clean sock
Small toys with different shapes (large enough not to choke on)

**Do**

Show and talk about the Bible Story Picture.

Show two toys to a child before putting them in a sock.

Ask the child to find a particular toy by reaching into the sock and feeling for it.

**Say**

The Bible tells us that God made our hands and feet. The little boy in this picture is touching the flower. The little girl is touching the water with her feet.

Colin, God made your hands. You can use your hands to find the ball. You did it!

God made your hands so that you can feel things. God made your hands so that you can play. God made all of you.

**Bonus Idea:** Children will enjoy using their hands to put items in and take items out of the sock.

## Where Is It?

**Collect**

Photos (from magazine or Internet) of body parts (face, hands, feet)
Laminating equipment or clear Con-Tact paper

**Do**

Before class, laminate pictures or cover them with Con-Tact paper.

In class, place them face down on a child-sized table or on the floor.

Ask one child at a time to choose a picture and turn it over.

**Say**

Sydney, you turned over the picture of the hand. Where is your hand? That's right! God made your hand. He gave you hands to hold things.

Let's see what other pictures we can find.

Evan, what picture did you turn over? You turned over a picture of feet. God made your feet. God made you.

## God Made Me Game

**Do**

Describe a child's hair color and clothing. Ask "Who is it?"

Guide other children to point to the child and say is or her name aloud.

**Say**

God made a girl with blond hair and green eyes. Who is it? Yes, it's Juliana! God made Juliana.

Who else did God make? God made a boy with brown hair and brown eyes. This boy is wearing a blue shirt. Who is it? You're right! God made Dominic.

Thank You, God, for making us.

# August

## God Gives Me Friends

### David and Jonathan Were Friends
(See 1 Samuel 18:1-4.)

### "Love each other."
(See John 15:12.)

**This month you will help each child:**

• hear songs and words about God's gift of friends;

• feel glad to be with his or her friends;

• play with toys and materials to learn about friends.

## Devotional

Take some time to read the story of David and Jonathan's friendship found in 1 Samuel 18—19:7. Notice how the circumstances of David and Jonathan's friendship changed drastically. At first, everything seemed rosy. Jonathan, King Saul, Saul's servants and all the people liked David. Friendship flourishes easily when things are going well.

But by the beginning of chapter 19, Saul's love for David has turned to raging jealousy. Now Saul seeks to turn Jonathan against David. Here comes the test of true friendship. Braving the wrath of his father the king, Jonathan stands up for his friend. It would have been so easy to bend, but Jonathan stood firm in the face of enormous pressure.

How strong are the friendships among the staff in your department? Are you merely acquaintances who happen to work together in the same room? Are you easily compatible only as long as everything runs smoothly? Or have you built relationships that help you sustain each other when pressure comes?

As you teach young children about friendships, nurture your relationships with the others who work with you. Pray for them, asking God's Spirit to knit your hearts together as He did the hearts of David and Jonathan.

During the month of August, display this poster at child's eye level. Talk about the way in which the children in the poster are showing that they are friends.

*Baby Beginnings® Teacher's Guide—18 to 36 Months* ●

### Do It!

I Roll the Ball

I roll the ball to you.
You roll the ball to me.
I can share the ball with you
Because we're friends, you see!

### Sing It!

Friends

(Tune: "Farmer in the Dell")

We can smile and wave.
We can smile and wave.
Because it's fun to be with friends,
We can smile and wave.

### Tell It!

David and Jonathan
Were Friends

David and Jonathan were friends.
They played like good friends do.
They helped each other, too.
Jonathan gave David his coat.
Jonathan said, "I love you."
"Thank you, Jonathan," David
said, "I love you, too."
God gives us friends, and we are glad.
(See 1 Samuel 18:1-4.)

Display this poster at teacher's eye level in your nursery. Tell the Bible story, sing the song, do the finger play and repeat the Bible verse to one or more interested children.

## Activities with Children

Choose one or more of the learning activities on pages 99-104 to provide for children during a session. Consider your facility, the number of children and teachers and the supplies you have available as you plan which activities you will use. The best kind of teaching for toddlers will happen as you take advantage of teachable moments as children play and experience the learning activities you have provided. Continue an activity as long as one or more children are interested. For more information on using this curriculum, see "Why Use Curriculum?" on page 8.

## Blocks and Friends

**Collect**

Large cardboard blocks

**Do**

Invite two children to work with you on a block structure.

Encourage sharing, helping and taking turns.

**Say**

It's fun when friends build together. God gives us friends to play with.

Hailey, I see that you have stacked two blocks. Now, Jackson is stacking a block. You are taking turns. Hailey and Jackson are friends.

Thank You, God, for our friends.

## I See Friends

**Collect**

Sand shovels and pails (optional—additional sand toys)

**Do**

Bring children outdoors to an enclosed sand play area.

Children play with sand toys.

**Say**

Julian, you are playing the sand with your friends today. What are your friends' names?

God gives us friends to play with. I see lots of friends here today. I see Julian, and Victoria and Sophie.

It's fun to play with our friends. We can share and help our friends.

**Bonus Idea:** Add a small amount of water to one or more watering cans. Help children pour small amounts of water in sand to play with.

## Find a Friend

**Collect**

August Bible Story Picture from *I Love to Look!* or *Nursery Posters*

**Do**

Show and talk about the Bible Story Picture.

Help a child hide in the room.

Have another teacher help other children to look for him or her.

Repeat with interested children.

**Say**

This is a picture of two friends. Their names are David and Jonathan. David and Jonathan helped each other. They were glad to be friends.

We have friends, too. Where is our friend, Elijah? There he is! Elijah is our friend. God gives us friends.

Let's see if we find another friend. We like to play with our friends.

## Rolling Along to You

**Collect**

One or more soft balls

**Do**

Sit on the floor with interested children.

Roll the ball to each in turn. If a child does not want to roll ball back, use another ball to continue play.

**Say**

God gives me friends. Alexis, you are my friend. I'll roll the ball to you. Dylan, you're my friend, too. Here comes the ball to you.

We are glad to play with each other. We are friends!

God gives us friends.

## God Gives Me Friends • Art and Sensory Play

## Sharing Play Dough

Note: This activity is best used with children over the age of two.

### Collect

Commercial or homemade non-toxic play dough

Fabric sheet or tarp

Masking tape

Items for making impressions in dough (jar lids, straws, sea shells, etc.)

### Do

Before class, tape sheet or tarp to floor under a child-sized table.

In class, give each child a fist-sized lump of dough. Carefully watch to be sure that children do not eat dough.

Help children flatten dough as needed. Children push items into dough to make impressions.

### Say

Paige, you are my friend. Let's play with play dough together. God gives us friends to play with.

Here is another friend! Here comes Daniel. Daniel wants to play with us, too.

I'm glad God gives us friends.

## Handprint Mural

### Collect

Length of butcher paper with space for all children to make handprints

Marker

Tape

Crayons

### Do

Print "God Gives Us Friends" at the top of the butcher paper. Tape paper on a child-sized table.

Help one child at a time place hand on paper while you trace around it in a color of the child's choosing. Print the child's name next to handprint. Child may decorate his or her handprint.

Fasten the paper to a bulletin board or wall for display.

### Say

Kennedy, there is your handprint. It's orange! Your handprint is right next to Colin's handprint. You and Colin are friends.

God gives us friends. We're glad to see our friends.

Thank You, God, for our friends Kenney and Colin.

**Bonus Idea:** Paint each child's hand with paint brush and let child make a handprint on the butcher paper.

## See Our Friends

### Collect

August Bible Story Picture from *I Love to Look!* or *Nursery Posters*

8½x11-inch (21.5x28-cm) sheet of card stock and one clear page protector for each child

Crayons

Photo of each child in the class, engaged in a learning activity

Glue

Marker

Three-ring binder

### Do

Show and talk about the Bible Story Picture.

Child uses crayons to decorate a page. Help child attach photo with glue. Write child's name on the page.

Place all children's pages in clear page protectors and put them in the binder. Keep binder in the classroom for children to look at. Be sure to include a page with your own picture.

### Say

God gives us friends. Here is a picture of two friends we read about in the Bible. Their names are David and Jonathan. Jonathan gave David a special coat.

We have some pictures of our friends at church. I see my friend Rebecca. I see my friend Lucas. You have lots of friends here today.

Friends love and help each other.

**Bonus Idea:** Take a class photo to insert into the binder.

## Find a Friend

**Collect**

August Bible Story Picture from *I Love to Look!* or *Nursery Posters*
Toy binoculars

**Do**

Show and talk about the Bible Story Picture. Encourage each child to "find a friend" by looking through the binoculars.

**Say**

Look at this picture. I see two friends: David and Jonathan. David and Jonathan were glad to be friends.

Lily, who can you see when you look through the binoculars? Yes! It's our friend Madeline. God gives you friends.

Let's count how many friends are here today. (Count children aloud.) Thank You, God, for all our friends.

## Friendship Cereal

**Note:** Post a note alerting parents to the use of food. Also, check children's registration forms for possible food allergies.

**Collect**

Several types of nutritious breakfast cereals without nuts, each placed into a small resealable plastic bag (one for each child)
Large bowl
Small bowl and spoon for each child

**Do**

Give each child a small bag with one kind of cereal in it. Explain that you are going to make "friendship cereal" today.

Help each child empty his or her cereal from bag to large bowl. Mix cereals together.

Scoop some cereal into each child's bowl. Children eat cereal.

**Say**

Let's make some cereal with our friends. God gives us good food to eat.

Joshua and Isabella have put their cereals into the bow. God gives us friends.

## Sea Shells

**Collect**

Variety of sea shells placed in a shallow basket or tray
Magnifying glass

**Do**

Children look at and touch sea shells. Interested children may use the magnifying glass to look at shells.

**Say**

Look at these shells God made. They come from the ocean.

Ethan, Hannah would like a turn with the magnifying glass. When you are done, can you give her a turn?

Thank you for sharing with your friend.

I'm glad God gives us friends.

**Bonus Idea:** Fill shallow plastic bowl part way with water. Children place shells in water to observe changes.

## Wind Watchers

**Collect**

Paper plates
Colorful crepe paper streamers
Stapler
Crayons

**Do**

Before class, staple three streamers to the side of each plate.

In class, children color plates. Then children hold the plates and wave them in the air. (Optional: Children run with plates in an enclosed outdoor play area.)

**Say**

James, I'm glad you are here with your friends today. When you and Kenna finish coloring on your plates, you can wave them together. It's fun to play with our friends.

I'm glad God gives us friends.

## Friendship Clap

**Collect**

*I Love to Sing!* CD and player

**Do**

Play "My Friends." Children clap hands to the music.

Encourage interested children to each hold a friend's hand and move in time to the music.

**Say**

I'm glad God gives us friends.

Let's say the names of our friends: Andrew, Olivia, Chloe and Tyler. Thank You, God, for all these friends.

## Hat Parade

**Collect**

*I Love to Sing!* CD (or other recorded music with a lively beat) and player

Variety of plastic or washable hats

**Do**

Let each interested child choose a hat to wear.

Play "Friends" or other music.

Lead a parade around the room.

**Say**

Let's have a hat parade today. All of our friends can wear hats and march together.

Which hat would you like to wear, Aidan? I'm glad you are my friend.

God gives us friends.

## Friendship Circle

**Collect**

August Bible Story Picture from *I Love to Look!* or *Nursery Posters*

**Do**

Show and talk about the Bible Story Picture.

Help children hold hands and form a circle. Sing the following words to the tune of "Are You Sleeping?":

Friends are walking, friends are walking.
Holding hands, holding hands.
Going in a circle, going in a circle.
All fall down, all fall down.

**Say**

The Bible tells us about two friends who loved each other. This is a picture of the two friends: David and Jonathan. They helped each other. God gives us friends who we can help.

We can make a circle with our friends. Let's listen to the music and walk in a circle.

God gives us friends at church. Thank You, God, for all of our friends.

## God Gives Me Friends

**Do**

When playing with children or eating snack together, sing the following words to the tune of "God Is So Good":

God gives me friends. God gives me friends.
God gives me friends. (Child's name)
is my friend.

**Say**

I'm glad God gives us friends.

God gives us friends to play with. God gives us friends to help us. We can help our friends, too.

Thank You, God, for the friends who are here today: Noah, Ella and Kaylee.

**Bonus Idea:** Sing "Who is my friend?" to the tune of "God Is So Good" while pretending to look around the room. Then sing song again using the name of a child: "Noah is my friend."

## Picnic with Friends

Note: Post a note alerting parents to the use of food. Also, check children's registration forms for possible food allergies.

**Collect**
Picnic basket or large grocery bag
Snack food, paper plates and napkins
Blanket

**Do**
Let children help put items in basket or bag.
Spread out a blanket on the floor and have a picnic. (Optional: Take children outdoors for a picnic in an enclosed play area.)

**Say**
Let's have a picnic with our friends. Adriana and Juan, can you sit down with me on the blanket?
I'm glad God gives us friends.
It's fun to eat with our friends.

## My Play House

**Collect**
Three sturdy adult chairs
Fabric sheet or lightweight blanket
Toys

**Do**
Before class, drape sheet or blanket over chairs, leaving one side entirely open.
In class, children play in the house with classroom toys. Talk about the times when you see two children in the house together.

**Say**
It's fun to go into our play house today. Maddie, you and Olivia are playing together in the house. Maddie and Olivia are friends.
I'm glad God gives us friends. Thank You, God, for our friends.

## Friendship Train

**Collect**
August Bible Story Picture from *I Love to Look!* or *Nursery Posters*
Child-size chairs

**Do**
Line up two or three rows of chairs with two chairs in each row.
Invite children to ride on the "friendship train."
Show and talk about the Bible Story Picture.

**Say**
Ava is sitting by her friend Brianna. They're pretending to go on a train ride.
God gives us friends. It's fun to play with friends.
Our friends at church are glad to be together. The Bible tells us about two friends who were glad to be together. Their names were David and Jonathan.
**Bonus Idea:** Give children paper rectangles to represent train "tickets."

## Driving to My Friend's House

**Collect**
Toy cars (with no small parts that children could choke on)
Shoe boxes with doors and windows drawn on them

**Do**
Place boxes a few feet apart.
Children "drive" their cars from house to house.

**Say**
I'm going to drive to my friend Alyssa's house. Hi, Alyssa! Do you want to play?
God gives us friends to play with.

## Friend Photos

**Collect**

Photo of each child

**Do**

Place all photos face down on a child-sized table.

Child turns over each photo one at a time.

Turn photos back over and repeat with interested children.

**Say**

Ethan, let's see if we can find the pictures of our friends. Can you turn over these pictures? Look, there is your friend Lauren.

God gives us friends. We have lots of friends here today.

Thank You, God, for all our friends.

**Bonus Idea:** Make a child-safe photo album of the children in your class. Children look at their pictures and pictures of friends.

## Peekaboo

**Collect**

Several sturdy paper plates

**Do**

When looking at a child, hold plate over your face.

Then remove plate while saying "Peekaboo!"

Let children hold plates over their faces, if interested.

**Say**

We can have fun playing with our friends. Let's play Peekaboo!

God gives us friends to play with. Friends can help each other.

We're glad to have good friends.

## Phone a Friend

**Collect**

Two toy telephones (or discarded real phones)

**Do**

Give one phone to a child.

Use the other phone yourself and talk to the child.

**Say**

Would you like to talk on the phone to me, Andrew? I'll call you on the phone. Hello, Andrew! I'm glad you're my friend.

God gives us friends. You can talk on the phone to your friend, too.

Friends love each other. Thank You, God, for our friends.

## Friendship Stories

**Collect**

August Bible Story Picture from *I Love to Look!* or *Nursery Posters*

Sturdy picture books showing children playing together

**Do**

Show and talk about the Bible Story Picture.

Read a book to one or two children at a time.

Look at the pictures and talk about the things the children are doing together.

**Say**

The Bible tells us about two friends. Their names were David and Jonathan. David and Jonathan helped each other. They were glad to be together.

The friends in this book are glad to be together, too. They are playing at the park. God gives us friends.

Friends have fun together.